Constructing
Kitchens

WILLIAM P. SPENCE

Sterling Publishing Co., Inc.
New York

DISCLAIMER

Although the information presented in the following pages was provided by a wide range of reliable sources, including material and tool manufacturers, professional and trade associations, and government agencies, it should be noted that the use of tools and materials in home-maintenance activities involves some risk of injury. The reader should also always observe the local building codes, the operating instructions of equipment manufacturers, and directions of the companies supplying the materials. The author and publisher assume no liability for the accuracy of the material included.

Library of Congress Cataloging-in-Publication Data

Spence, William Perkins, 1925-
   Constructing kitchens / William P. Spence.
      p. cm. -- (Building basics)
   Includes index.
   ISBN 0-8069-8105-9
    1. Kitchens--Design snd construction. 2. Kitchens--Remodeling.
   I. Title. II Series.
TH4816.3.K58 S64 2001
643'.4--dc21   00-048261

Designed by Judy Morgan
Edited by Rodman Neumann

1 3 5 7 9 10 8 6 4 2

Published by Sterling Publishing Company, Inc.
387 Park Avenue South, New York, N.Y. 10016
© 2001 by William P. Spence
Distributed in Canada by Sterling Publishing
c/o Canadian Manda Group, One Atlantic Avenue, Suite 105
Toronto, Ontario, Canada M6K 3E7
Distributed in Great Britain and Europe by Cassell PLC
Wellington House, 125 Strand, London WC2R 0BB, England
Distributed in Australia by Capricorn Link (Australia) Pty Ltd.
P.O. Box 6651, Baulkham Hills, Business Centre, NSW 2153, Australia
Printed in China
All rights reserved

Sterling ISBN 0-8069-8105-9

Contents

Kitchen Design Principles

If you are planning a kitchen for a new home, you have more freedom than if you are remodeling an existing kitchen. With new construction you can still change the size and shape of the area. A remodeling job presents fixed walls which, while they can be moved, increase the cost of the job (**1-1**). It is also more difficult to relocate electrical connections and plumbing in a remodeling job. Once the kitchen appliances and cabinets are installed the arrangement of the room is

Courtesy Lithonia Lighting

1-1 Remodeling an existing kitchen usually requires you to work with the existing size and shape of the area. The kitchen is typically combined with a dining area and sometimes includes a snack bar for quick meals.

fixed, whereas other rooms permit you to move furniture about and even change their use. So good planning at the start is very important.

In both situations you must meet local codes such as electrical and plumbing requirements. Ventilation is another factor to be considered.

Appliances and cabinets are manufactured in a wide range of sizes, so you must begin to make some decisions on the types and brands to be used. This information is needed so you can plan the layout. Cabinets can also be custom built to fit your situation. The appliances must fit into the overall design and have the accessories you desire, such as an icemaker. There are many types of sink made from several different materials and in a number of sizes. They influence the space needed for installation.

Frequently the kitchen is combined with a dining area or at least a snack bar for quick meals. It also may open onto a family room with a television, sofa, and space for hobby activities and other family activities. The kitchen provides for food storage and preparation, cooking, baking, utensil storage, china and silverware storage, linen storage, and dining.

NATIONAL KITCHEN & BATH ASSOCIATION

Many of the design recommendations in this chapter and in parts of other chapters were developed from those in various National Kitchen and Bath Association publications, with their permission. The National Kitchen and Bath Association is a professional organization representing over 7,000 industry professionals across the United States and Canada, including manufacturers and their products, dealers, and designers. For more on the NKBA, see the section on additional information, on page 155.

WORK AREAS

Kitchen planning involves providing for a pattern of work flow for storing, processing, and cooking food as well as serving the prepared items and cleaning up after meals. The basic kitchen is planned around three major appliances that include the **cooking/baking unit**, a **refrigerator/freezer**, and the **dishwasher** near one or more sinks (1-2).

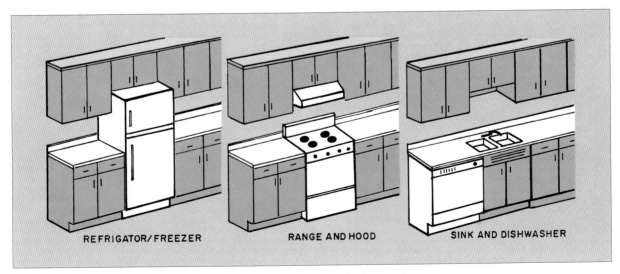

REFRIGATOR/FREEZER   RANGE AND HOOD   SINK AND DISHWASHER

1-2 The kitchen is planned around three major appliances and adjacent fixtures.

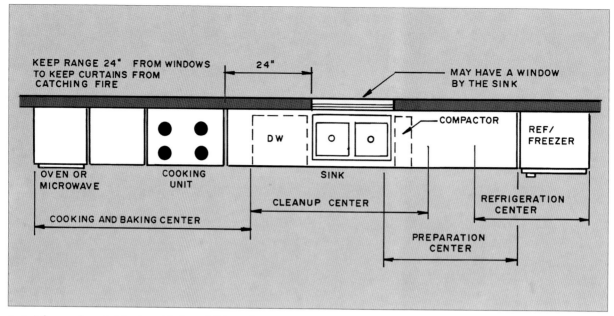

KEEP RANGE 24" FROM WINDOWS TO KEEP CURTAINS FROM CATCHING FIRE

24"

MAY HAVE A WINDOW BY THE SINK

COMPACTOR

DW

REF/ FREEZER

OVEN OR MICROWAVE

COOKING UNIT

SINK

CLEANUP CENTER

REFRIGERATION CENTER

COOKING AND BAKING CENTER

PREPARATION CENTER

1-3 The work activities in a kitchen fall into four major areas. These are closely related and are the key to planning a satisfactory kitchen.

Courtesy Whirlpool Corporation

1-4 The cooking center is where food is boiled, baked, fried or broiled. Notice the microwave located above the range. While this is convenient the microwave can be located in other areas of the kitchen.

Related to the three appliances, there are four work activities that are the key to kitchen design: cooking/baking, cleanup, preparation and mixing, and refrigeration (shown for the I-shaped kitchen in **1-3**). Notice these activities overlap; counter space is an important consideration.

As you plan these work areas consider other appliances that may be installed, such as a microwave, compactor, dishwasher, or freezer.

THE COOKING/BAKING CENTER

The cooking center is where the food is heated, broiled, baked, or fried (**1-4**). Since food generally leaves it and goes to the dining area, it helps if it is near it to make serving easier. The cooking unit and oven are the major appliances, and possibly a microwave could be here. A number of cooking appliances are available, including cooktops, separate ovens, and a range with one or two ovens in a single appliance. The cooking center should be near the food preparation area. If you have ovens separate from the cooking unit they can be some

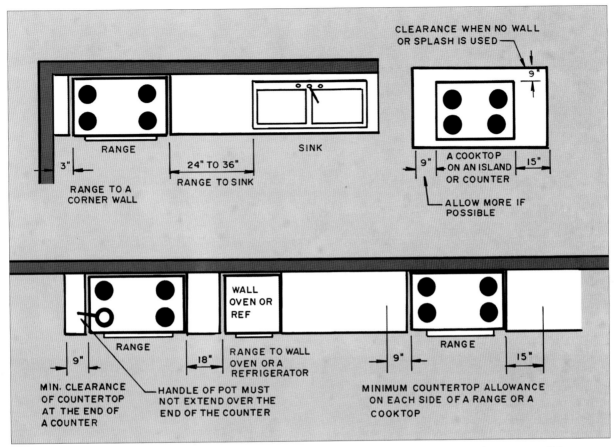

1-5 Minimum countertop allowances beside the cooking unit. Increase these amounts whenever possible.

distance away because they are not heavily used and once the food is in the oven it does not require constant attention. The microwave should be within the cooking work area because food items go in and out of it rapidly. Microwaves are typically mounted in a wall cabinet, so this will reduce storage at the range.

Remember to place a hood over the cooking unit to remove cooking fumes and water vapor developed. It is helpful if you provide storage for the cooking utensils within the cooking area. Counter space needs to be planned to accommodate small appliances such as coffeemakers, teamakers, toasters, and broilers. These require a number of electrical outlets along the wall in the cooking area.

It is important to allow open countertop space beside the range or cooktop so you have a place to put pans and food being cooked. Typical minimum spacing requirements are in 1-5. As you plan the layout of the kitchen, try to exceed these minimum distances.

LOCATING THE MICROWAVE

The microwave oven is used frequently for meal preparation. Consider locating it near the refrigerator. There is little relationship between the microwave and the oven or range so they need not be in the same area.

The bottom of the microwave should be 24 to 48 inches above the floor. This makes it easy to use. The microwave oven can be mounted on

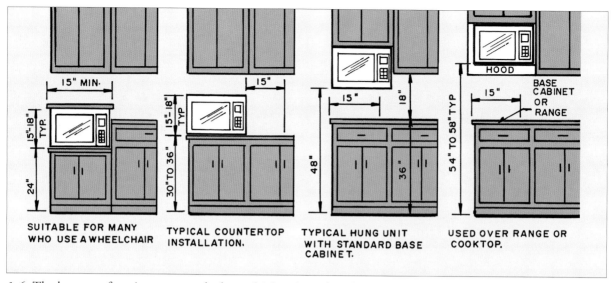

Within the diagram:

SUITABLE FOR MANY WHO USE A WHEELCHAIR

15" MIN.

15"-18" TYP.

24"

TYPICAL COUNTERTOP INSTALLATION.

15"

15"-18" TYP.

30" TO 36"

TYPICAL HUNG UNIT WITH STANDARD BASE CABINET.

15"

18"

48"

36"

USED OVER RANGE OR COOKTOP.

HOOD

15"

BASE CABINET OR RANGE

54" TO 58" TYP

1-6 The bottom of a microwave can be located 24 to 48 inches above the floor. Allow at least 15 inches of clear counterspace beside, above or below the unit.

1-7 A microwave can be located above a range or cooktop, but there is a risk of getting burned if something is cooking on them.

CONSTRUCTING KITCHENS

base cabinets or hung from the wall as shown in **1-6**. Allow at least 15 inches of counter space above, below, or beside the unit. Some home owners or contractors prefer mounting the microwave oven on a special hood that is designed to vent the range and carry the weight of the microwave. This is an acceptable location, as seen in **1-4** and **1-7**. However, there is a danger of getting burned from cooking taking place on the range below as you reach over it to open the microwave.

REFRIGERATION CENTER

The refrigeration center is where frozen foods and other food items that need to be kept cold but not frozen are stored (**1-8**). The refrigerator/freezer unit is a frequently used appliance, so plan its location to be convenient to the preparation and cooking centers. It is also an important part of the storage plan. You should allow clear countertop space of at least 15 inches on the latch side of the refrigerator. If it has a vertical freezer and the unit has two doors, put 15 inches on each side. You

Courtesy Congoleum Corporation

1-8 The refrigerator/freezer is the major appliance in the refrigeration center. This center has both base and wall cabinets, providing good storage. Notice that the resilient floor covering blends in with the wall color.

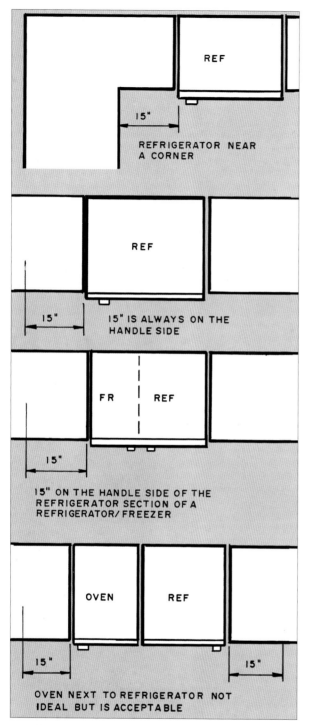

1-9 Minimum countertop allowances beside the refrigerator/freezer.

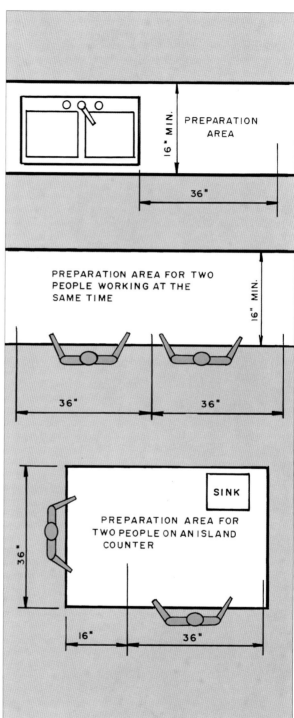

1-10 Minimum countertop allowances for the food preparation center.

CONSTRUCTING KITCHENS

need this surface to place foods going into and being removed from the unit. Spacing recommendations are shown in **1-9**.

THE PREPARATION CENTER

The preparation center is where foods are mixed, vegetables cleaned, and other steps are taken for preparing food. Minimum space recommendations are shown in **1-10**. This area should be near the sink and refrigerator. It requires enough counter space to hold the food and utensils required. If you do a lot of baking and preparation of raw foods and meats, you will want to plan a longer counter (**1-11**).

1-11 This sink serves as the center of the area for preparing food for cooking and serving. It has clear countertop on both sides, providing needed space.

THE CLEANUP CENTER

The cleanup center is where the pots and pans are cleaned and dishes, silverware, and storage containers are rinsed and given a thorough washing. The sink is the major item and usually a double sink is installed (1-12).

The dishwasher is located next to the sink so it is easy to place dishes in it. Locate it on the left of the sink for right-handed persons or to the right of the sink for left-handed persons (1-13). The trash compactor will be placed on the side opposite the dishwasher.

A disposal may be installed in the sink to grind up and dispose of soft items. The switch to operate it should be far enough away from it so that a person could not have fingers in the unit and turn it on at the same time.

Some prefer to place the sink by a window (see the kitchen shown in 1-19). While this is pleasant, it is not necessary. A light may be placed on the bottom of the cabinet over the sink and provides excellent lighting (see Chapter 6). The sink can be placed along a wall, on a peninsula, or on an island. It is important to give it a central location because it is also used frequently when cooking. Some like to install a second sink in large kitchens to have one near both the storage and cooking areas.

Provisions for recycling and disposing garbage and dry trash are part of the planning that is needed as you lay out the cleanup center. These are typically part of the base cabinet forming the cleanup center.

Recommendations for locating a primary sink in relation to the dishwasher and providing clear countertop for cleanup and preaparation adjacent to the primary sink and a secondary kitchen sink are shown in 1-14.

1-12 The sink is the center of the cleanup area. Counterspace on both sides is necessary. The dishwasher is next to the sink. A trash compactor could be added on the other side of the sink.

Courtesy GE Appliances

1-13 The dishwasher is located beside the sink.

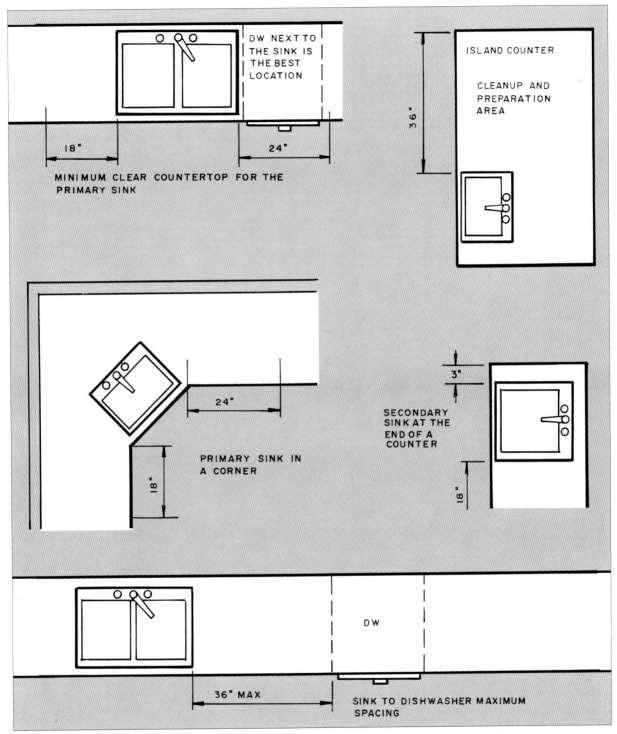

DW NEXT TO THE SINK IS THE BEST LOCATION

18"

24"

MINIMUM CLEAR COUNTERTOP FOR THE PRIMARY SINK

36"

ISLAND COUNTER

CLEANUP AND PREPARATION AREA

24"

18"

PRIMARY SINK IN A CORNER

3"

SECONDARY SINK AT THE END OF A COUNTER

18"

36" MAX

DW

SINK TO DISHWASHER MAXIMUM SPACING

1-14 Other minimum spacing recommendations for the primary and secondary kitchen sinks.

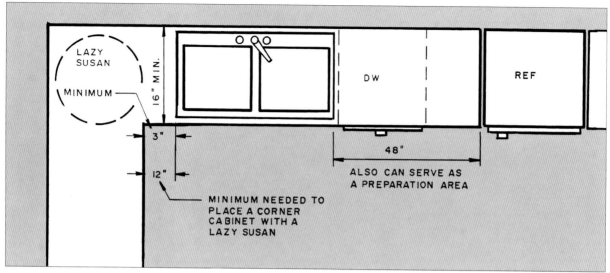

1-15 When a sink is near a corner of the cabinets locate it at least 3 inches away. The countertop between the sink serves as a cleanup area and part of the refrigeration area. The length will be the recommended 36 inches plus an extra 12 inches since it serves both areas.

Recommendations for locating the sink in relation to appliances and activities along one arm of an L-shaped counter are shown in **1-15**.

If a corner cabinet with a lazy Susan is planned, you will need a minimum of 12 inches between the edge of the sink and the corner of the base cabinet with the lazy Susan. A typical installation of a sink adjacent to a corner-cabinet lazy Susan is shown in **1-16**.

When two work centers are adjacent, as are the sink and refrigerator in **1-15**, the minimum countertop required will be the longest of the recommended counter lengths for one of these plus 12 inches.

1-16 This installation has a corner base cabinet with a lazy Susan installed next to a sink.

STORAGE

Storage is required for packaged and fresh foods, frozen foods, kitchen accessories, utensils, dishes, silverware, electrical appliances, linens, cleaning supplies, brooms, mops, and other such items. A large house will require more storage space than a small house and will typically have a larger kitchen and dining area. Typical minimum storage recommendations made by the National Kitchen and Bath Association are in **Table 1-1**.

In **1-17** is a typical layout for a kitchen having less than 150 ft². If wall space is short an island counter could be used instead of the peninsula. A layout for a kitchen with more than 150 ft² is in **1-18**.

As you plan your storage space, you want to locate items such as utensils and food products as near as possible to the work center where they will be used. Take advantage of the many features offered by cabinet manufacturers to utilize

TABLE 1-1 RECOMMENDED MINIMUM STORAGE CAPACITY

	Kitchen 150 ft² or less	Kitchen larger than 150 ft²
Base cabinet frontage	156 in.	192 in.
Wall cabinet frontage	144 in.	186 in.
Drawers (individual total frontage)	120 in.	165 in.

Courtesy National Kitchen and Bath Association

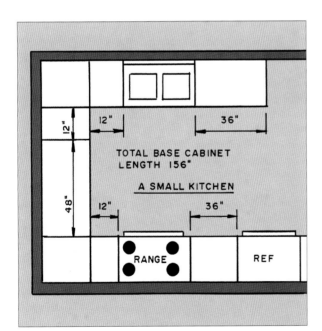

1-17 A typical base cabinet layout for a kitchen with less than 150 ft². It has the minimum lineal inches of base cabinet storage space. The cabinets must be at least 21 inches deep.

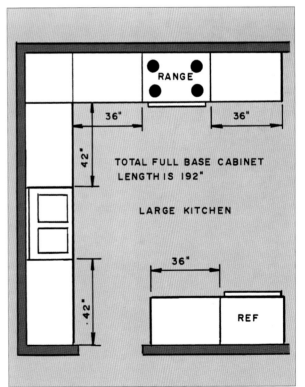

1-18 A typical base cabinet layout for a kitchen having more than 150 ft² of floor space. This plan provides the minimum lineal inches of storage. The cabinets must be at least 21 inches deep.

the space available most efficiently. These include things such as adjustable shelves, pull-out shelves, various wire racks, and adjustable inserts. The use of shallow shelves for small items such as spices can free up a standard-width shelf for larger items. Provide a number of shallow drawers rather than a couple of deep drawers. See Chapter 3 for details.

Food storage involves frozen foods, foods requiring cold storage, and a wide range of canned and dried foods (**1-19**). The refrigerator-freezer is a part of the overall storage plan. While the freezer section usually will not hold large quantities of food, a separate freezer can be located elsewhere in the house. Typically a basement or garage location is used.

Canned and dried foods are stored in wall and base cabinets. Cabinet manufacturers have a number of specially designed units that help store the variously shaped and sized products efficiently. Consider adding a pantry, which is a small closet. It will hold a large number of dried, canned, and fresh items, such as potatoes and onions.

Locate the major food storage area near the door through which the items will enter the house as you bring them from the store.

RECYCLING

Many families actively participate in recycling programs, so it is wise to provide some storage for handling these waste products. You need to

1-19 Food, utensils, china, silver, linens, and other items are stored in wall and base cabinets and placed near the work center where they will be used.

store cans, glass, plastic bottles, and newspapers. Special bins can be built for these items in the cabinets. These tend to collect in the cleanup center and require an additional 2 or 3 feet of base cabinet.

WASTE DISPOSAL

Considerable waste material is developed every day, including wet materials that will decompose and many dry items suchas napkins and boxes. A garbage disposal will handle most wet material but some do not want one for fear of clogging the sewer line.

Some means of receiving this waste and easily disposing of it needs to be incorporated into the kitchen cabinet design.

A compactor is a good way to handle dry solid waste that you do not want to recycle. It is placed on one side of the sink. The kitchen seen in **1-19** has a compactor to the left of the sink.

PLANNING AREA

Some enjoy having a small desk or low cabinet to use as a place for planning meals, handling household finances, and taking care of general correspondence. This can be built in the kitchen in an area outside the work triangle. The top should be desk height, which is usually 30 inches (**1-20**).

DINING AREA

Many people want a small dining area in the kitchen for breakfast and noon snacks. This can be an area for a small table and chairs (**1-21**) or a counter that

1-20 A planning area is a very useful part of a kitchen. Since it is not directly involved in food preparation or cleanup it can be placed in a less accessible area.

1-21 A small dining area in a section of the kitchen is a popular feature. The light color of the resilient flooring enhances the dark cabinets and dining furniture.

may be a peninsula or island unit with stock (**1-22**). Recommended table sizes for seating two to six people are shown in **1-23**. Spacing recommendations for tables are shown in **1-24**.

The peninsula and island eating area can vary in height from a low of about 19 inches to a high of 42 inches. The height of the eating counter together with the allowance for knee space are the factors that determine the nature of the seating. Some require a tall stool while others can use a normal chair as shown shown in **1-25**. The seating chairs or stools can also be used to determine the best height and spacing of the counter you are designing. Allow at least 24 inches of countertop for each position at the peninsular or island eating counter (see **1-26**, on page 20). Booths are also popular. Typical sizes are given in **1-27**, on page 20.

1-22 This island counter serves as a dining area and provides a work surface during the food preparation process. The resilient tile floor is durable and will withstand the use of the chairs.

CONSTRUCTING KITCHENS

1-23 Suggested minimum table sizes for seating 2 to 6 people.

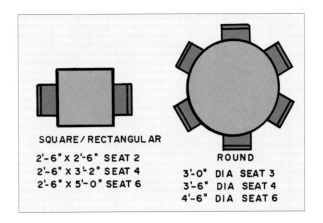

SQUARE / RECTANGULAR

2'-6" X 2'-6" SEAT 2
2'-6" X 3'-2" SEAT 4
2'-6" X 5'-0" SEAT 6

ROUND

3'-0" DIA SEAT 3
3'-6" DIA SEAT 4
4'-6" DIA SEAT 6

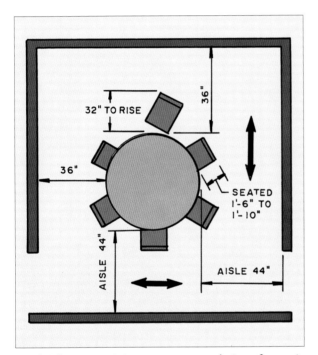

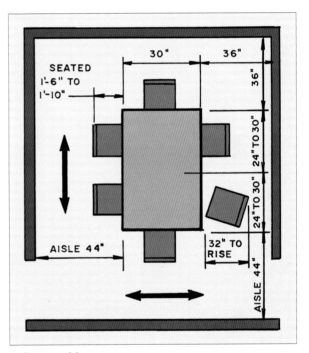

1-24 These are minimum recommendations for seating at a dining table.

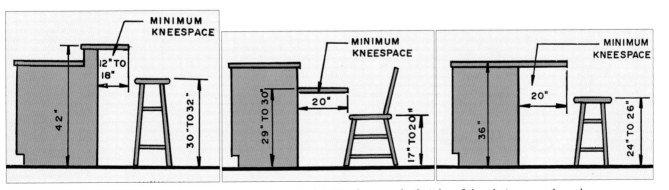

1-25 The height of eating counters can be varied. This changes the height of the chair or stool used.

KITCHEN DESIGN PRINCIPLES

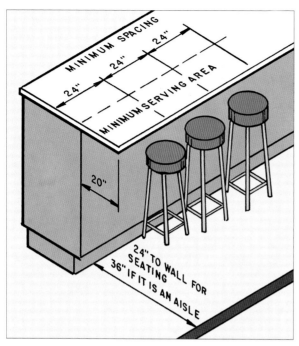

1-26 An eating counter should provide at least 24 inches of clear countertop for each person and adequate kneespace below the top.

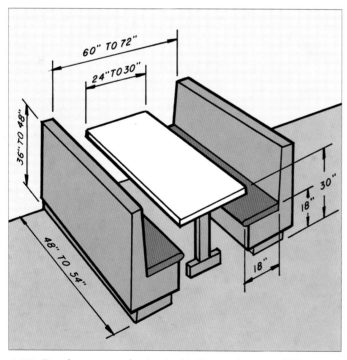

1-27 Booths are popular in the kitchen eating area. These are typical sizes for a booth to seat four people.

OTHER CONSIDERATIONS

After you have prepared a drawing of your proposed solution, begin consideration of some other features such as required plumbing, electrical needs, wall and floor finish, and the type of countertop. Your cabinet dealer will have several styles of cabinet available made from a number of different woods and constructed in different ways, such as with and without a faceframe.

THE WORK TRIANGLE

The concept of the work triangle has been used for many years as a means for checking the efficiency of a kitchen. This is the total straight-line distance from the refrigerator to the stove to the sink. This is the distance you would walk as you move between these three appliances. Typically each side of the triangle should fall between 5 to 10 feet. The total of all three sides will average out around 22 to 26 feet (**1-28**). This total can be somewhat larger or smaller than this, but it is best if it is in this range. Likewise if one side is very short, less than 5 feet, the appliances are too close together and may be difficult to use, especially if two people are working in the kitchen.

When you add a second sink or plan a large kitchen for two cooks working at the same time, you will have to vary the distances somewhat and possibly plan two work triangles (**1-29**).

If the kitchen is very large, you can use an island counter or a peninsula to shorten the distances between work centers. The island counter or peninsula may allow you to have two triangular paths or a set of paths with more than three sides. However, the goal is to access the work centers with the minimum number of steps (**1-30** and **1-31**).

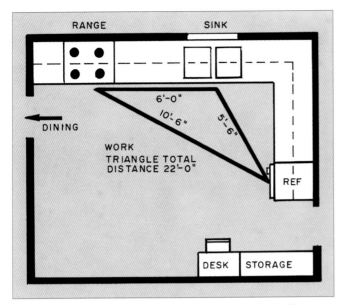

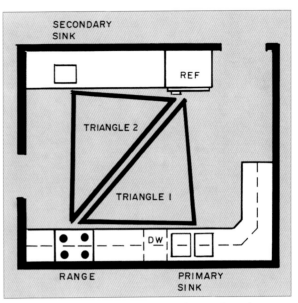

1-28 This L-shaped plan shows a typical small kitchen with an adequate work triangle. The work triangle is used to check the efficiency of the plan.

1-29 This kitchen added a secondary sink and was arranged with two work triangles, enabling two people to work at the same time.

1-30 An island counter can be used to reduce the size of the work triangle, thus reducing the number of steps between the work areas.

1-31 The peninsula counter can have a sink or range, thus shortening the distance between work centers. It can also serve as an eating area. (Courtesy Aristokraft, Inc.)

KITCHEN DESIGN PRINCIPLES

Also be aware that traffic flow through the kitchen should not cross any of the sides of the work triangle. For example, someone entering the house through a door from the garage and passing through the kitchen should not interfere with someone preparing a meal. Can you get a drink from the refrigerator without getting in the way of the cook? Maybe you can place the refrigerator near the edge of the triangle.

It is recommended that the distances between appliances in the work centers be as follows: sink to refrigerator 4 to 7 feet, sink to range 4 to 6 feet, range to refrigerator 4 to 10 feet. An efficient layout is shown earlier in 1-28.

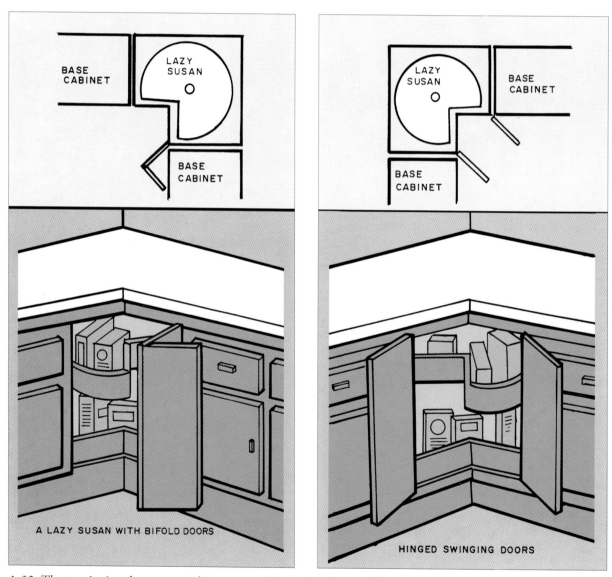

1-32 These swinging doors are used on corner cabinets that form a 90° corner.

CONSTRUCTING KITCHENS

USING CORNERS

Most kitchen layouts have the cabinets turn corners—creating a large dead area that can be put to good use with proper planning. The countertop in the corner provides a large surface that might be useful for locating small appliances. The base corner cabinets can be designed to make the space useful by including a lazy Susan in the design. It may have swinging doors (**1-32**) or have the doors attached to the lazy Susan as shown in **1-33** and earlier in **1-16**. You can build the cabinet so that it is on a diagonal across the corner and place a lazy Susan inside (**1-34**).

1-33 The lazy Susan may have the doors attached so that they rotate with it.

1-34 Some corner cabinets are built with a 45° diagonal face. They use a lazy Susan and a swinging door.

Another way to handle the problem of a corner is to use a corner cabinet with a diagonal front and place a primary or secondary sink in the countertop (**1-35**). If you install a dishwasher, move it far enough over so the door can open while you stand in front of the sink.

Wall cabinets are usually only 12 inches deep, so it is easier to reach into them at the corner.

Some common ways to install wall cabinets forming a 90° corner are shown in **1-36**. A corner wall cabinet with a diagonal face and a lazy Susan is the one of the best ways to use the corner (**1-37**). If you have a base cabinet with a diagonal front you must use a diagonal corner wall cabinet. Otherwise you cannot reach the back of the wall shelf in the corner (**1-38**).

Courtesy Subzero Freezer Co., Inc.

1-35 A sink can be built into a corner cabinet having a diagonal front. A 12- or 15-inch base cabinet is inserted between the corner cabinet and a dishwasher so you can open its door while standing at the sink. Notice the use of cabinets for storage at the sink.

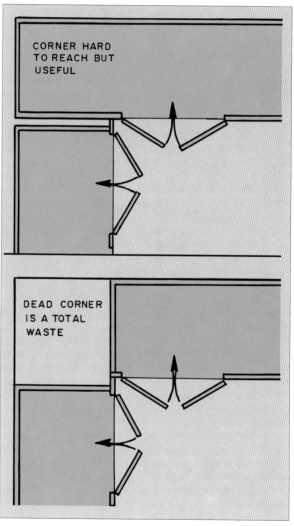

CORNER HARD
TO REACH BUT
USEFUL

DEAD CORNER
IS A TOTAL
WASTE

1-36 Common ways to install wall cabinets at a 90° corner.

CONSTRUCTING KITCHENS

1-37 This corner wall cabinet has the face built on a diagonal and a lazy Susan inside.

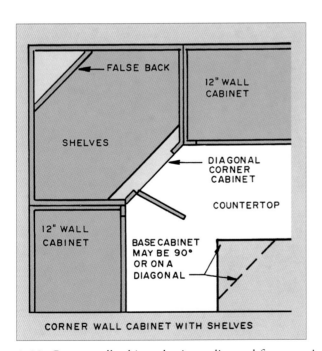 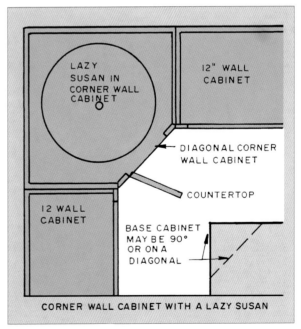

1-38 Corner wall cabinets having a diagonal face permit you to install a lazy Susan, which makes the area more easily accessible.

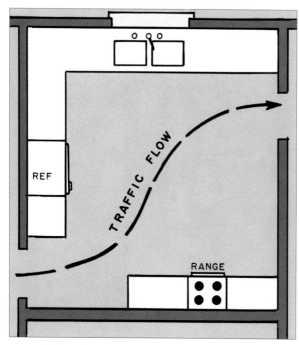

1-39 When the primary traffic flow is through the center of the kitchen it can disrupt food preparation activities.

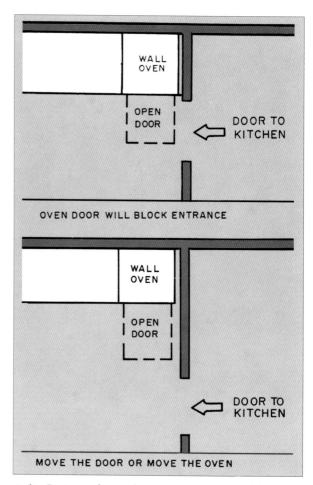

1-40 Position the appliances so they do not block the entrance into the kitchen.

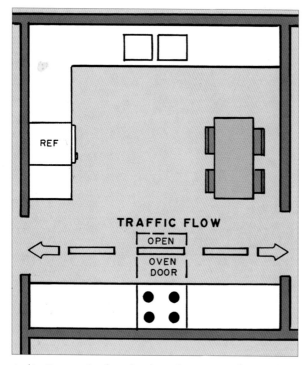

1-41 Be certain that the door from an appliance does not interfere with the flow of a primary traffic aisle.

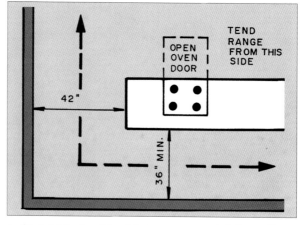

1-42 A 36-inch-wide aisle is recommended for traffic flow past a counter where no appliance is to be used. If aisles intersect, one should be at least 42 inches wide.

TRAFFIC PATTERNS

When you locate the kitchen on the floor plan you must consider certain traffic patterns to reach it and possibly through it. For example, it is typical to place the kitchen next to the garage. This makes it easier to move food into the kitchen and to carry out the waste. However, you may have caused a traffic flow pattern through the work triangle to reach the rest of the house from the garage (**1-39**). Also be careful you do not block the flow into the kitchen by opening appliance doors (**1-40**). Traffic flow should not interfere with someone working in the kitchen.

You need to consider the impact of major traffic flow through the kitchen as you locate the appliances. A major flow of traffic should not go past major appliances, as shown in **1-41**. A traffic aisle along the side of a counter where no appliance will be used should be 36 inches wide. When aisles meet at 90°, one should be at least 42 inches wide. This will also allow a person in a wheelchair to make the turn (**1-42**).

VENTILATION

Adequate ventilation in a kitchen is very important. The cooking activities generate moisture, fumes, grease in the air and odors that eventually cling to the cabinets, walls, curtains, flooring, and other exposed items. Range hoods and exhaust fans are commonly used to disperse these pollutants.

Range hoods remove the pollutants and exhaust them to the outdoors. They also provide a source of light on the range. There is a wide range of designs and colors. They can match your appliances and provide an attractive covering over the range (**1-43**).

1-43 Range hoods remove cooking fumes and disperse them to the outdoors. They are available to match the range or cooktop.

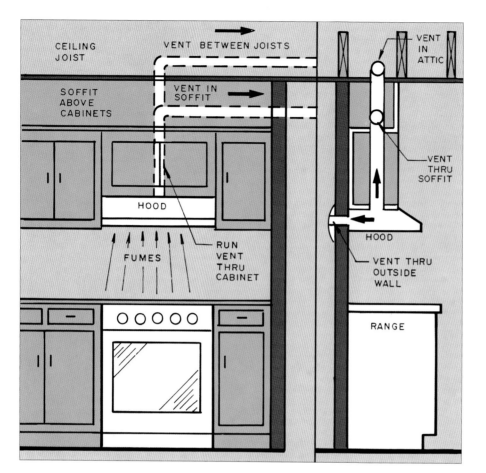

CEILING JOIST

VENT BETWEEN JOISTS

SOFFIT ABOVE CABINETS

VENT IN SOFFIT

HOOD

FUMES

RUN VENT THRU CABINET

VENT IN ATTIC

VENT THRU SOFFIT

HOOD

VENT THRU OUTSIDE WALL

RANGE

1-44 You can vent a range hood through the attic joists, inside the wall cabinet soffit, or, if on an outside wall, directly through the wall.

1-45 This hood supports a microwave over a range and is ductless. It filters the air and returns it to the room.

Range hoods have aluminum mesh filters that trap grease and are removed and cleaned with normal detergents. They have a blower that lifts the smoke and fumes and vents them to the outdoors. The vent is a pipe that is typically run into the attic and then between the joists to the exterior or through the furred-down soffit above the cabinets (**1-44**). If it is a remodeling job and you cannot use these areas for a vent, you could use a **ductless hood** (**1-45**). These hoods move the fumes through an activated charcoal carbon filter or an aluminum screen filter that must be cleaned regularly as per the manufacturer's instructions. The hood seen in **1-45** is this type, and it also holds a microwave.

Hoods are also used over cooking surfaces that are on islands as well as over indoor gas-fired barbecue units (**1-46**).

A range hood or other venting device should have a fan rated at 150 cubic feet per minute.

Courtesy Wellborn Cabinet, Inc.

1-46 Hoods are used on island cooking surfaces and gas-fired barbecues.

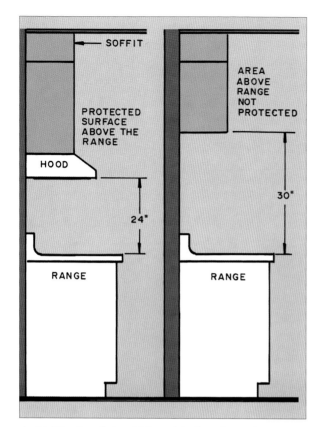

1-47 The hood should be 24 inches above the range. If no hood is used, raise any cabinets above it to 30 inches.

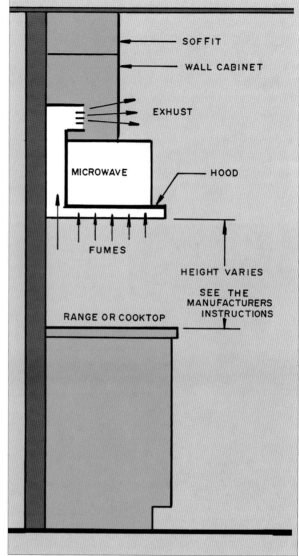

1-48 The clearance needed by ductless hoods and those carrying microwaves should be spaced as directed by the manufacturer.

1-49 (Left) This cooktop has several heating elements of different sizes and a downdraft ventilation grill in the center that eliminates the need for a hood.

The distance between the surface of the cooking unit and the ventilation hood should be 24 inches (1-47). If no ventilation hood is used, the cabinets over the cooking area should be at least 30 inches above the range (1-47). If you use a hood carrying a microwave, the height will vary. You need to observe the manufacturer's recommendations (1-48).

Another type of range vent is a **downdraft system** that is part of the cooktop (1-49). A horizontal opening beside the burners with a fan below draws the fumes in and exhausts them outside through a duct. Another type has a small panel across the back of the range. As it tilts or rises from the burner surface, a fan is activated. When the vent is lowered it shuts off (1-50).

Another type of range ventilation is a through-the-wall exhaust fan. The range has to be placed along an exterior wall. The fan is mounted on or in the wall above the stove (1-51). This system is not widely used anymore, since the range hood is more effective.

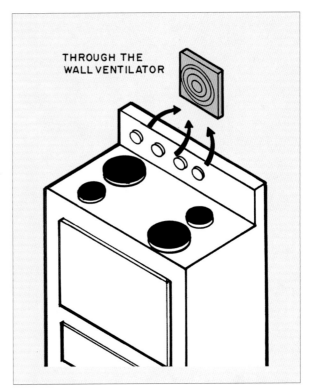

1-51 Exhaust fans above the range pull fumes from the cooking and vent through the exterior wall.

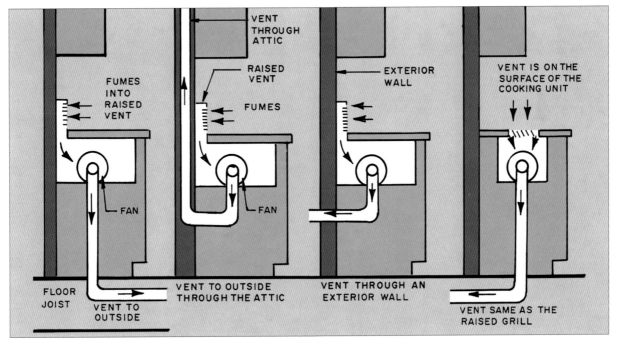

1-50 A downdraft cooking venting system pulls the fumes from the cooking surface and exhausts outdoors.

ACCESSIBLE WORK CENTERS

There are many things you can do to increase the accessibility of the various work centers in a kitchen. Sizing the cabinets and providing adequate floor space help those who are wheelchair users. Better lighting and larger lettering can help those with poor eyesight. Using pulsating light signals instead of the typical buzzer will help those who have hearing problems. Careful attention to the physical limitations of home owners will produce a kitchen in which they can function successfully and safely.

Begin by planning the layout so someone in a wheelchair may work comfortably in the kitchen. Doors into the kitchen should be at least 32 inches. However, this is minimum, and a 36-inch door is much better. Since a wheelchair has a turning circle of 60 inches, arrange the cabinets and appliances so it can be maneuvered to access each work center. This is relatively easy to do in **L-shaped** (1-52) and **U-shaped** (1-53) kitchens. If the cabinet has a recessed area, this could be used as part of the turn area. A corridor kitchen is used in small houses, so a 60-inch-wide aisle is not always available. If you have a large opening under the

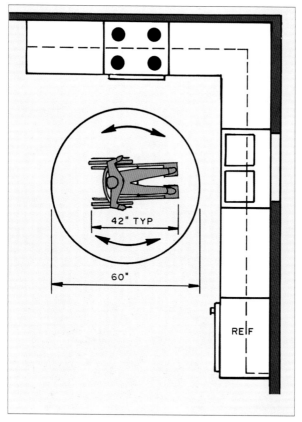

1-52 An L-shaped kitchen provides easy access to the appliances and cabinets for someone in a wheelchair.

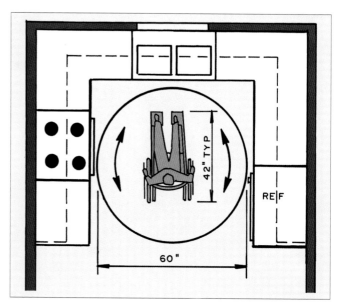

1-53 The U-shaped kitchen is easy to arrange for someone in a wheelchair if the cabinets are spaced to allow an easy turn between cabinets.

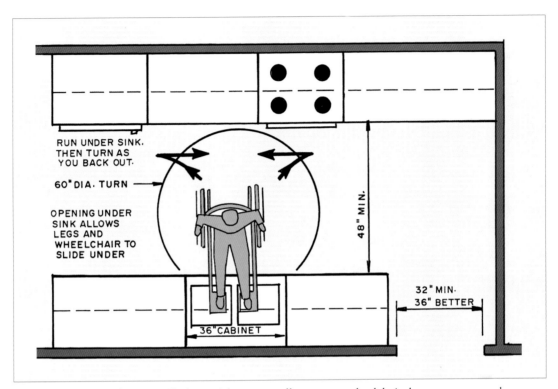

RUN UNDER SINK.
THEN TURN AS
YOU BACK OUT.

60" DIA. TURN

OPENING UNDER
SINK ALLOWS
LEGS AND
WHEELCHAIR TO
SLIDE UNDER

48" MIN.

32" MIN.
36" BETTER

36" CABINET

1-54 Corridor kitchens usually have aisles too small to turn a wheelchair, but you can use the space under an open counter or appliance to give room to back out and turn.

counter, such as at the sink or preparation area, the wheelchair can run up under the counter and back out right or left. If you have a 48-inch-wide aisle, this makes a tight but possible turn (1-54). These principles can be applied to kitchens of any configuration. Specifications for making buildings accessible by the physically handicapped are available in report ANSI-A117.1 of The American National Standards Institute, Inc., 11 West 42nd St., 13th Floor, New York, N.Y. 10036 and in the Americans with Disabilities Act.

As you plan the cabinets, remember that the highest shelf that can be reached straight forward from a wheelchair is 48 inches (1-55). To reach the bottom shelf of wall cabinets you will have to put them about 12 inches above a 36-inch-high counter. The lowest shelf that can usually be reached is 9 inches above the floor.

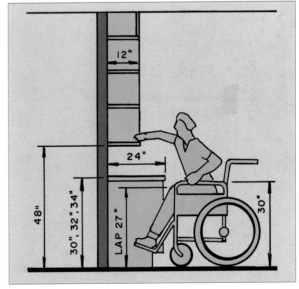

12"

24"

48"

30", 32", 34"

LAP 27"

30"

1-55 A person leaning forward from a wheelchair can reach about 48 inches above the floor. Therefore the bottom shelf of wall cabinets should be 48 inches above the floor.

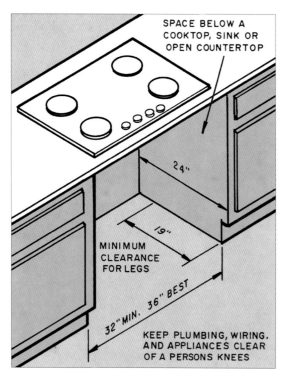

1-56 Building an opening below a counter allows the person in a wheelchair to reach near the back of the counter.

Those using wheelchairs have difficulty reaching across the countertop. For example, it is difficult to reach the faucet handles. Therefore you need to open the cabinet below the sink and any countertops, such as in the food preparation area, and below the cooking unit. The opening should be at least 30 inches wide and 24 inches deep (1-56). It is necessary to move the water and waste lines below the sink. Run them down the wall and cover with plywood or drywall so the person using a wheelchair does not hit them (1-57). Be certain the controls on the cooking unit are on the front edge so the person does not have to stretch across the burners to reach them.

Knee space can also be provided beside a wall oven or microwave to make such appliances accessible. The door should open down or at least away from the side with the knee space (1-58).

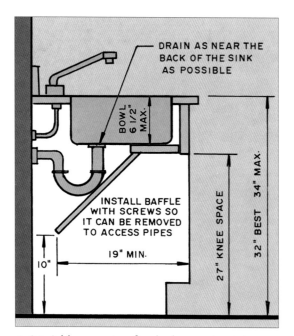

1-57 Add protection for the legs under sinks. Reroute the drain and water lines to clear the area as much as possible.

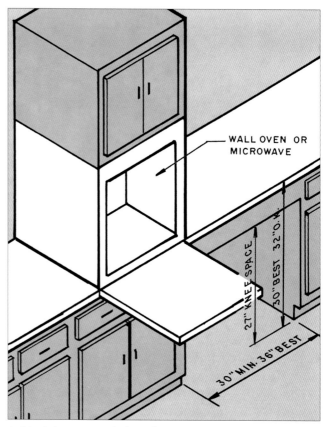

1-58 A knee space below the countertop is needed beside wall ovens and microwaves.

Base cabinets are available that can be lowered to a 30-inch height (**1-59**). Wall cabinets are also available that can be raised or lowered on wall-mounted tracks to the desired height (**1-60**). Since these may be raised above the standard cabinet heights they are very useful for persons who are taller than average and need a higher sink and higher shelving.

Cabinets having sliding shelves instead of fixed shelves is of great help to everyone.

Courtesy GE Appliances

1-59   Base cabinets are available where the height of a sink or range can be adjusted to a height suitable for someone in a wheelchair or someone who is tall and wants the appliance higher than the standard cabinet.

WALL CABINET AT NORMAL HEIGHT

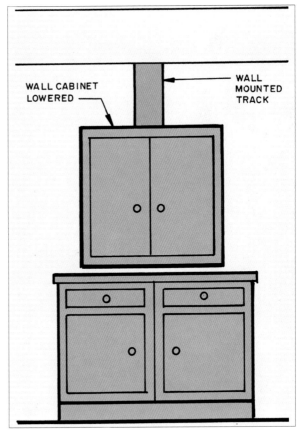

WALL CABINET LOWERED

WALL MOUNTED TRACK

1-60   Wall cabinets that mount on a track on the wall are available. They can be raised or lowered to the height desired.

KITCHEN DESIGN PRINCIPLES

Basic Kitchen Shapes

The rooms in a typical home are generally either rectangular or nearly square. When designing a new house you might consider planning how you would like a kitchen and dining area and arrange the walls to accommodate the plan. In any case, kitchens tend to fall into a number of rather standard shapes. These include an **L-shaped** kitchen, **U-shaped** kitchen, a double **L-shaped** kitchen, a **G-shaped** kitchen, an **I-shaped** kitchen, and a **corridor** kitchen. These shapes can be altered and enhanced a little by adding an island counter or a peninsula.

Keep in mind that a small kitchen should have at least 130 lineal inches of open countertop and a large kitchen could have 200 lineal inches or more.

Courtesy G.E. Appliances

2-1 This L-shaped kitchen has an oven in the corner cabinet and a cooktop and microwave around the corner. Notice the doors on the refrigerator match those on the cabinets.

L-SHAPED KITCHEN

The **L-shaped** kitchen has cabinets and appliances along two butting walls forming a corner (**2-1**). If the cabinets on one wall are very long and the other short, the efficiency is reduced. This kitchen leaves a large open floor area which could be used for dining or other activities. The layouts shown in **2-2** have the work triangle below 22 feet.

The efficiency can be improved by adding an island counter as shown in the lower diagram in **2-2** and seen in **2-3**, on page 38. The island can be used for a range, cooktop, or sink. It can also provide a surface for a small dining or snack area.

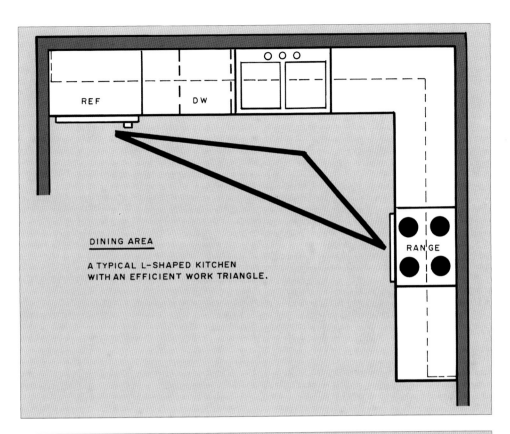

DINING AREA

A TYPICAL L-SHAPED KITCHEN
WITH AN EFFICIENT WORK TRIANGLE.

REF DW RANGE

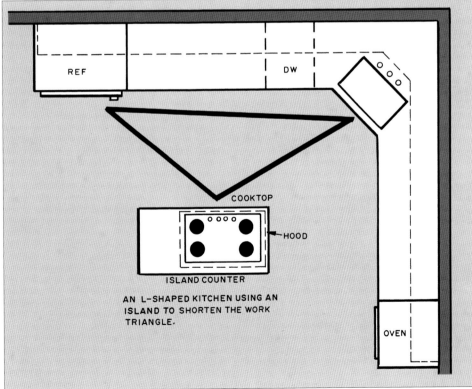

REF DW

COOKTOP

HOOD

ISLAND COUNTER

AN L-SHAPED KITCHEN USING AN
ISLAND TO SHORTEN THE WORK
TRIANGLE.

OVEN

2-2 L-shaped
kitchen layouts
can provide for an
efficient kitchen.
Notice one uses an
island counter.

U-SHAPED KITCHEN

A **U-shaped** kitchen has cabinets on three sides of the room. Arranging cabinets in this way reduces the walking distance between the work centers, producing an efficient kitchen. A small dining area can be located on the open side. The U-shape can be formed using a peninsula counter on one side instead of a wall (**2-4**). Some typical plans are shown in **2-5**, and in **2-6**, on page 40. If two people are to work in the kitchen, be certain the aisles are wide enough to allow easy access to the appliances.

Courtesy Whirlpool Corporation

2-3 This L-shaped kitchen places a cooktop on an island counter, reducing the distance between the work centers. Notice the placement of the appliances.

Courtesy Wellborn Cabinet, Inc.

2-4 A U-shaped kitchen is very efficient.

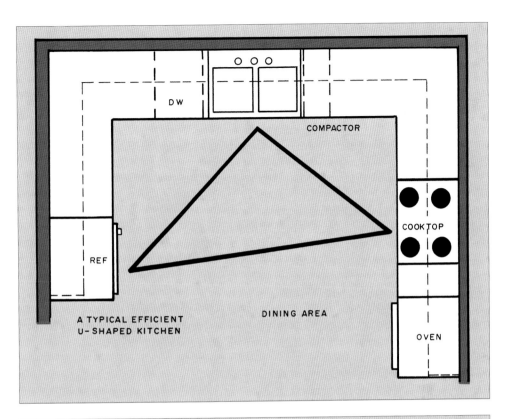

A TYPICAL EFFICIENT
U-SHAPED KITCHEN

DINING AREA

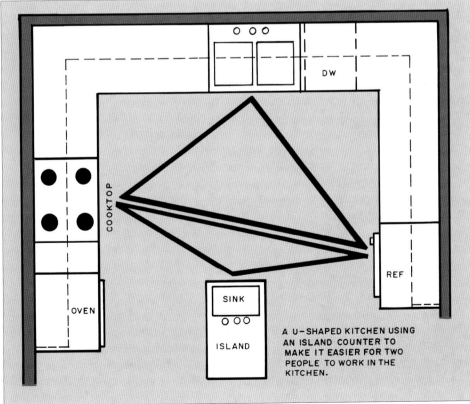

2-5 Typical layouts for U-shaped kitchens. Notice an island is used in one to make it easier for two people to work at the same time in the kitchen.

A U-SHAPED KITCHEN USING
AN ISLAND COUNTER TO
MAKE IT EASIER FOR TWO
PEOPLE TO WORK IN THE
KITCHEN.

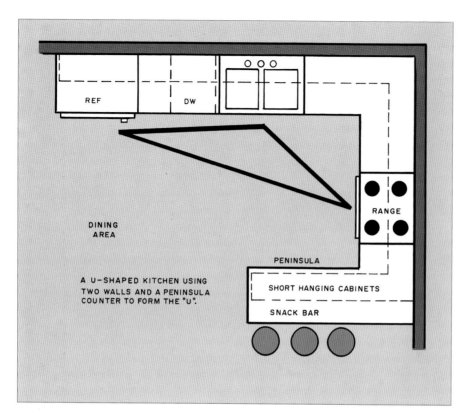

REF

DW

RANGE

PENINSULA

SHORT HANGING CABINETS

SNACK BAR

DINING
AREA

A U-SHAPED KITCHEN USING
TWO WALLS AND A PENINSULA
COUNTER TO FORM THE "U".

2-6 Another layout for
a U-shaped kitchen uses
a peninsula counter to
provide a small dining
area.

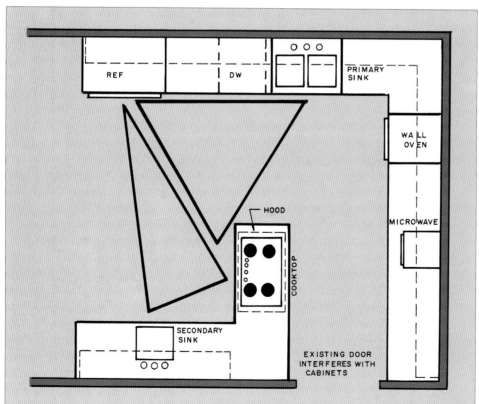

REF

DW

PRIMARY
SINK

WALL
OVEN

MICROWAVE

HOOD

COOKTOP

SECONDARY
SINK

EXISTING DOOR
INTERFERES WITH
CABINETS

2-7 A double
L-shaped kitchen
can help make a
useful layout when
a window, door, or
other obstruction
interferes with the
cabinets along the
wall.

CONSTRUCTING KITCHENS

DOUBLE L-SHAPED KITCHEN

A **double L-shaped** kitchen is a useful design if you want a **U-shaped** kitchen but a door or window interferes with the layout. It will involve developing two work triangles which can be effective if you add a secondary sink in a convenient location. A typical example is shown in **2-7**.

G-SHAPED KITCHEN

The **G-shaped** kitchen is efficient but requires that the cabinets be spaced far enough apart so two people can work at the same time. It can be formed using the fourth wall of a kitchen or installing a peninsula across the end of the open side of the U-kitchen as shown in **2-8**. One typical layout is shown in **2-9** and a second in **2-10**, on the following page.

Courtesy Merillat Industries, Inc.

2-8 This G-shaped kitchen runs a peninsula counter with a second sink off the stone wall on one side of the kitchen.

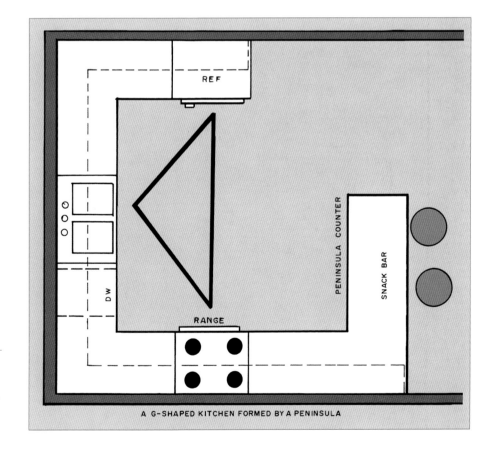

2-9 A G-shaped kitchen can add additional cabinet space and sometimes shorten the work triangle.

REF

DW

RANGE

PENINSULA COUNTER

SNACK BAR

A G-SHAPED KITCHEN FORMED BY A PENINSULA

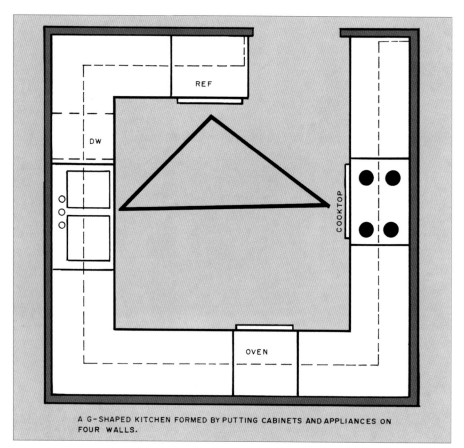

REF

DW

COOKTOP

OVEN

A G-SHAPED KITCHEN FORMED BY PUTTING CABINETS AND APPLIANCES ON FOUR WALLS.

2-10 Another G-shaped kitchen layout, shortening the work triangle and separating the oven from the cooktop.

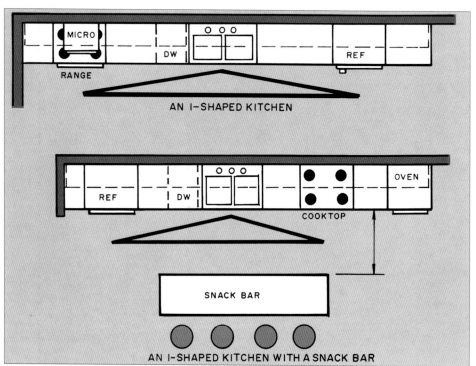

MICRO

RANGE

DW

REF

AN I-SHAPED KITCHEN

REF

DW

COOKTOP

OVEN

SNACK BAR

AN I-SHAPED KITCHEN WITH A SNACK BAR

2-11 The I-kitchen stretches along one wall and is suitable for use by only one person.

I-SHAPED KITCHEN

The **I-shaped** kitchen has the appliances and cabinets along one wall. It is used in small apartments and small houses. All of the utilities are in one wall. The problem is trying to get everything you need along the wall without its getting too long. Typically it will only let one person work in the area. Two examples are shown in **2-11**. A shortage of clear countertop makes it difficult to have a place to put everything. Basically it is useful for those who do very little food preparation but of little use for the person who likes to cook.

CORRIDOR KITCHEN

The **corridor** kitchen has appliances and cabinets on two opposite walls. It can be used when space for a kitchen is limited to a long narrow area. It can be designed to have a short work triangle and is an efficient design. However, it is difficult for two people to work in it at the same time. Some typical examples are shown in **2-12**. You have to be especially careful that you do not place appliances with doors directly across from each other. With the minimum width between walls, open appliance doors will cause some difficulty.

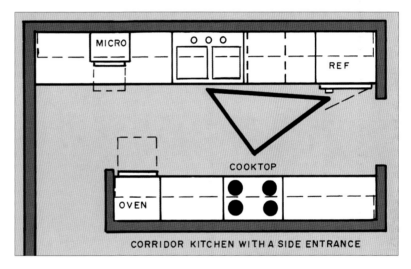

CORRIDOR KITCHEN WITH A SIDE ENTRANCE

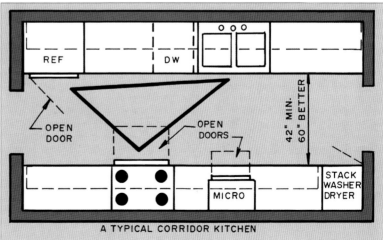

A TYPICAL CORRIDOR KITCHEN

2-12 The corridor kitchen can be built in a long narrow space. While it is efficient to use, generally only one person can work in it.

Courtesy Whirlpool Corporation

2-13 This kitchen occupies a large area and uses an island to carry the cooktop to make the work triangle effective. A small dining area is connected to the island. Notice how the finishes on the appliances are coordinated, providing an attractive kitchen.

Courtesy Congoleum Corporation

2-14 This kitchen has a peninsula counter extending out from the wall, providing additional storage and serving as a room divider. The walls have been painted to blend with the resilient floor covering.

ISLAND COUNTERS & PENINSULAS

Island counters are freestanding units allowing a means for adjusting the work triangle, providing additional storage, or serving as a small dining area. They can contain a sink or appliances. In a large kitchen a second sink is often located here. An island counter with a cooktop and dining area is in **2-13**.

A **peninsula** is a section of counter connected on one end to the cabinets along the wall. It goes across the open end of the kitchen forming a divider to the next room, which might be for a dining or a family room. It can be used to hold a sink, range, cooktop, storage space, extra surface for work or dining (**2-14**).

SPECIAL KITCHENS

Creative architects often produce floor designs for kitchens other than the typical square or rectangular room. The room may have a curved wall, a wall of glass, or walls that meet at angles other than 90°. This flexibility permits the kitchen designer to be creative in producing a plan that will be meet or exceed the minimum spacing requirements.

In **2-15** the kitchen has a very irregular shape with cabinets flowing back into an area with large windows. This requires a number of corner cabinet units. The effect of this nook is to produce a visually pleasing kitchen area. Actually, rather than a kitchen, the room has the look of a pleasant family room.

2-15 This cabinet installation has to turn a number of corners to flow into the small area in the back with the windows. The warm wood produces a pleasant atmosphere.

Courtesy G.E. Appliances

2-16 This kitchen is pie shaped and an island counter containing cooking and dining facilities slopes parallel with the sides of the room.

Courtesy G.E. Appliances

2-17 This kitchen is very unusual and because of the sloping walls and gleaming appliances gives a bright, interesting appearance.

CONSTRUCTING KITCHENS

The kitchen in **2-16** is wider at one end, so the island counter has been tapered to match the slope of the walls.

The kitchen seen in **2-17** I consider to be a great kitchen. The side walls are on angles and the end wall makes an acute angle. Notice how the appliances have been worked in with the cabinets to produce an exciting kitchen.

Custom-built cabinets can providing considerable storage as shown in **2-18**. This configuration also holds a refrigerator unit up off the floor so that it is easy to access. The refrigeration unit can be installed in cabinets such as these or set back in walls, allowing access to it wherever refrigerated storage is needed.

In **2-19** the "kitchen look" is diminished by placing a colorful sofa up against an island counter that contains a sink. The white wood framing and cabinets flow easily into the white refrigerator/freezer. The bright wall colors also diminish the look of a typical kitchen.

In **2-20** a special effort was made to give the kitchen the appearance of a more formal room.

2-18 This custom made cabinet provides considerable storage and holds a refrigeration unit at a height that makes it easy to use. The antique finish on the cabinet helps diminish the appearance that it is part of the kitchen.

The dark cabinets with considerable detailing including paneling, the use of cabinets with glass doors, and the use of wallpaper all contribute to the pleasant appearance.

2-19 Creative planning was used to hide an island counter with this bright sofa and to coordinate the wall colors with it. The refrigerator and cabinets blend together, forming a unified whole.

2-20 This kitchen does not have the "kitchen" look but a more formal appearance. The dark hardwood cabinets contribute to this impression. Notice the paneled island counter and small dining table with classic Queen Anne legs.

CHAPTER 3

Cabinets & Countertops

Cabinets are divided into several large groups including wall cabinets, base cabinets, vanity cabinets, tall cabinets, and utility cabinets (3-1). The main components making up these units are drawers, doors, faceframes, shelves, unit sides, backs and bottoms, bases, tops, and hardware.

Manufactured cabinets are produced in three general categories: stock, semi-custom, and custom. **Stock cabinets** are standard mass-produced units built in large numbers and stored until a dealer needs them. They typically will have particleboard sides, back, and bottom and solid wood faceframes, drawer fronts, and doors. They

Courtesy Lithonia Lighting

3-1 Typical units of the kitchen cabinet system include wall cabinets, base cabinets, utility cabinets, and tall cabinets that are complemented by a choice of countertop and backsplash.

TABLE 3-1 TYPICAL TESTS OF THE KCMA CERTIFICATION PROGRAM

Type of Test*	Component	Number of Tests	Purpose
Structural	Cabinetry	Five	to measure the cabinet's structural integrity and installation
Mechanical	Doors	Two	to test door operation and to measure durability
	Drawers	Two	to test the ease of drawer operation and to measure durability
Abrasive	Finish	Five	to test finish coating for resistance and durability

*Additonal requirements must be met for materials, construction techniques, design characteristics, and hardware utilized

are made in standard sizes based on a 3-inch increment in width.

Semi-custom and **custom** cabinets bought from a dealer are also mass produced by a cabinet manufacturer. They are made to the size and specifications of the home owner. The local cabinet dealer will work out what is wanted on a particular job and send the information to the manufacturer. Since these are built only when an order is received, delivery takes longer, so plan ahead if you are going to use them. The manufacturer will build your cabinets to the size and shape you specify. However, you will have to choose from the various door- and drawer-front designs they use.

Generally, semi-custom and custom cabinets use more expensive woods and better construction methods than stock cabinets. There could be a difference in the quality of the hardware. Because of these and the extra labor required, they cost more than stock cabinets. However, stock cabinets are of excellent quality and often it is difficult to tell them apart from semi-custom and custom cabinets. If the cabinets are certified by the Kitchen Cabinet Manufacturers Association, you know they meet rather stringent standards.

CERTIFIED CABINETS

The Kitchen Cabinet Manufacturers Association (KCMA) operates a certification program that assures the specifier and user of kitchen cabinets and bath vanities that the cabinets bearing their blue and white seal comply with the rigorous standards set by the American National Standards Institute (ANSI) and sponsored by the KCMA. The cabinets are subjected to a number of tests, as shown in **Table 3-1**. In addition there are many requirements to be met relating to the materials, construction techniques, design characteristics, and hardware.

The hardware used must meet the standards in ANSI/BHMA A156.9 (American National Standards Institute/Builders Hardware Manufacturers Association).

Complete details of the certification program are available in the publication ANSI/KCMA A161.1. Publications are available from the Kitchen Cabinet Manufacturers Association. See "Additional Information" on page 155 for the address and other related trade and professional organizations.

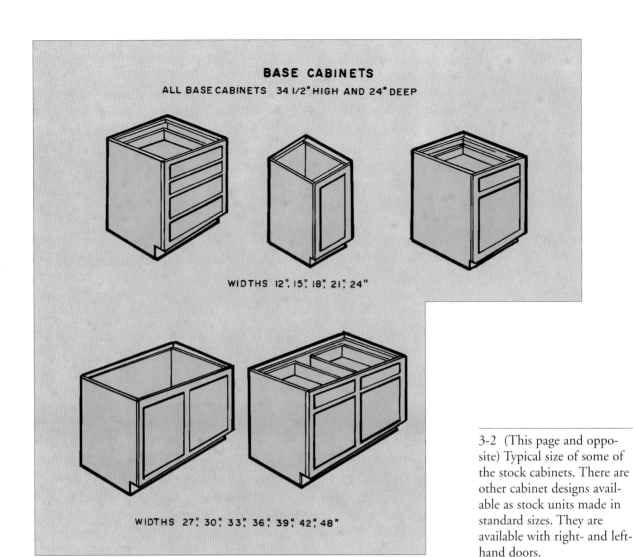

BASE CABINETS
ALL BASE CABINETS 34 1/2" HIGH AND 24" DEEP

WIDTHS 12", 15", 18", 21", 24"

WIDTHS 27", 30", 33", 36", 39", 42", 48"

DIAGONAL CORNER WALL CABINET
HEIGHTS 30 1/2", 36 1/2", 42 1/2"

24"
24"
12"

3-2 (This page and opposite) Typical size of some of the stock cabinets. There are other cabinet designs available as stock units made in standard sizes. They are available with right- and left-hand doors.

STOCK CABINET SIZES

Stock cabinets are built in a variety of heights and widths as well as styles. The widths are on 3-inch increments. Some of the commonly available sizes are shown in **3-2**. Consult your cabinet dealer to verify the sizes of cabinets that are available from the manufacturers they represent. This information will prove very helpful as you locate the appliances on the kitchen layout and fill in the planned cabinet area with specifically sized base and wall cabinets.

SINK BASES
34 1/2" HIGH 24" DEEP

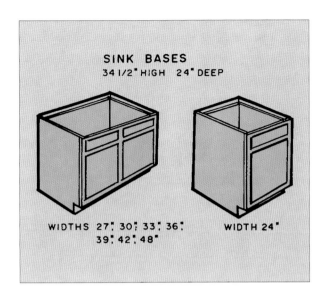

WIDTHS 27", 30", 33", 36",
39", 42", 48"   WIDTH 24"

SINK FRONTS

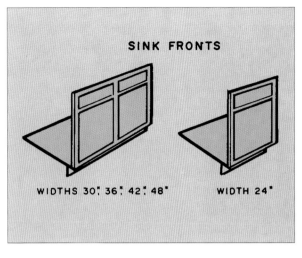

WIDTHS 30", 36", 42", 48"   WIDTH 24"

TALL CABINETS
12" AND 24" DEEP

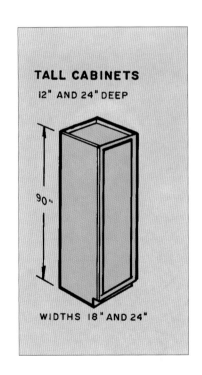

90"

WIDTHS 18" AND 24"

WALL CABINETS
HEIGHTS 12", 15 1/2", 18 1/2", 24 1/2", 30 1/2"
DEPTH 12"

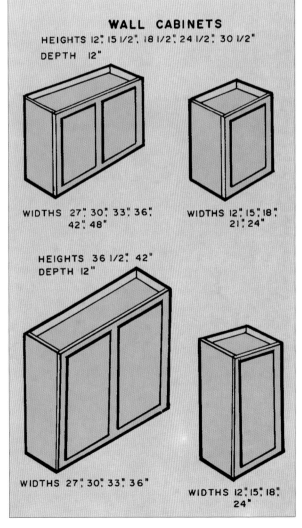

WIDTHS 27", 30", 33", 36",
42", 48"   WIDTHS 12", 15", 18",
21", 24"

HEIGHTS 36 1/2", 42"
DEPTH 12"

WIDTHS 27", 30", 33", 36"   WIDTHS 12", 15", 18",
24"

3-3 This base cabinet has a wide faceframe.

FACEFRAME & FRAMELESS CABINETS

Manufactured and custom-built cabinets are available with and without a faceframe. Those with a faceframe are most widely used. A typical cabinet with a faceframe is shown in **3-3**. Some typical construction details are shown in **3-4**. In most examples of cabinets the sides and bottom will be ½-inch to ⅝-inch particleboard with a ¼-inch hardboard or plywood back. The faceframe is typically made of ¾-inch solid wood.

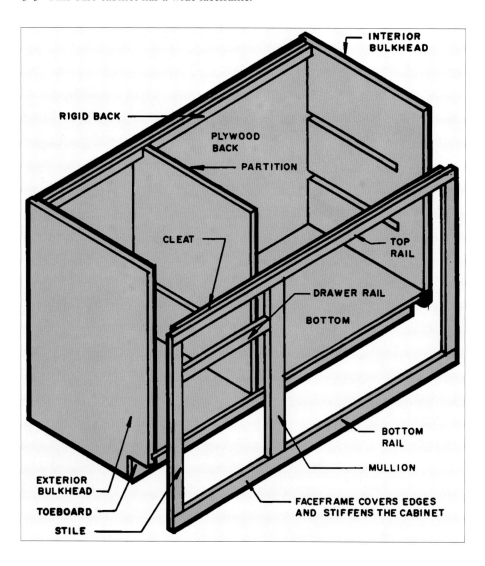

3-4 These are typical construction details for a the carcass of a base cabinet with a faceframe.

CONSTRUCTING KITCHENS

The frameless cabinet does not have a face-frame. It is modeled on a European-style unit often based on a repeating 32mm unit (see the section following on the 32mm system). Since the frameless cabinet does not have a faceframe, the carcass has to use ¾-inch particleboard sides and bottom. The back is ¼ or ⅜-inch plywood. It provides the strength to keep the carcass from racking. A frameless cabinet is shown in **3-5**. Typical carcass construction is shown in **3-6**.

3-5 A cabinet using frameless construction.

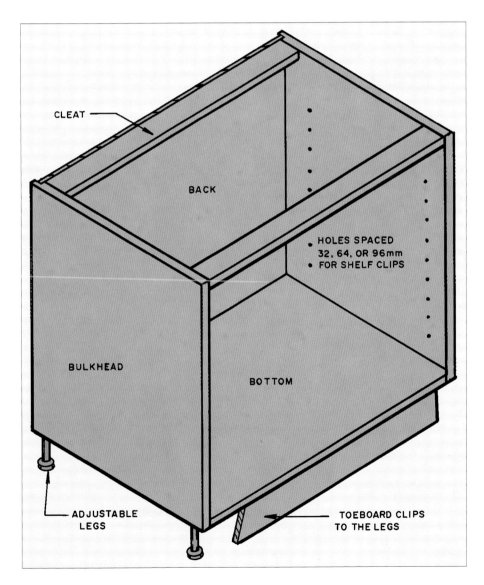

3-6 Here are typical carcass construction details for a base cabinet using frameless construction.

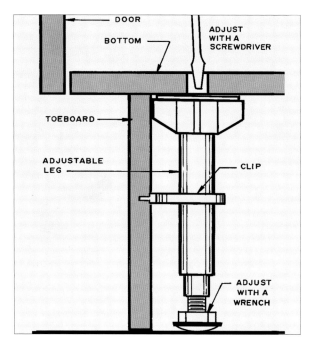

One type of frameless cabinet manufactured has metal legs to which a kickboard is clipped. Their length is adjusted with a screwdriver from inside the cabinet or with a wrench on the nut at the end on the floor, as shown in 3-7.

32mm SYSTEM

Cabinets with a faceframe are often referred to as "traditional cabinets," whereas frameless cabinets are sometimes called "European cabinets." This is simply because frameless construction first became popular in Europe; however, since the frameless construction is based on a repeating 32mm unit, professional cabinetmakers refer to this as the 32mm system.

3-7 (Above) The length of the legs on European-style cabinets can be adjusted with a screwdriver or a wrench.

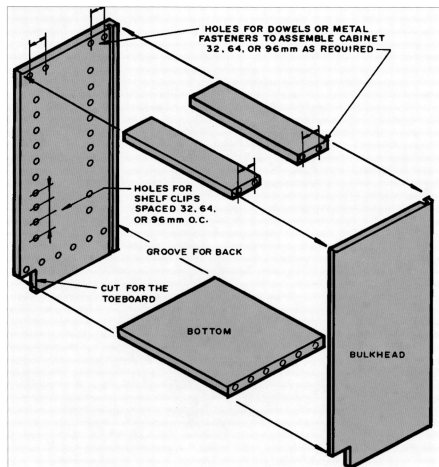

3-8 (Right) European style cabinets are assembled with dowels spaced in the butting members 32mm on center.

The 32mm system produces cabinets using flat panels and standardized measurements in increments of 32mm. The cabinet is joined by drilling dowel holes spaced 32mm apart, center to center, along the butting edges of the carcass. These are drilled with a multiple-spindle drilling machine so that all the holes in one piece are drilled at the same time. Likewise the shelves are adjustable and sit on pins in rows of dowel holes spaced 32mm on center. A typical carcass is shown in **3-8**.

This system uses precision woodworking machinery that permits fast setups and accurate machining. Specially designed hardware enables cabinets to be produced faster and at less cost than conventional methods using a faceframe.

DOORS

Cabinets with faceframes may have doors that have a lip, are flush, or are overlaid (**3-9**). **Lipped doors** were widely used for many years but are not used much today. The rabbeted edge for the lipped door is on all four sides; in order to close the drawer properly, the faceframe opening must be absolutely square.

FLUSH DOORS

Flush doors are set inside the faceframe in the same manner that full-size doors are set in your house. The faceframe opening must be square and the door made accurately or it will not close. These are not widely used for cabinets.

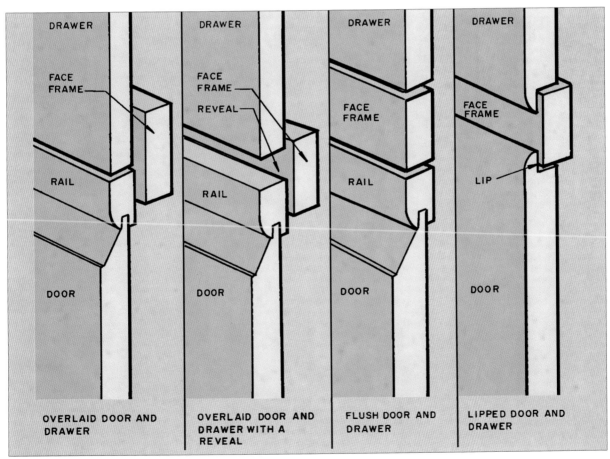

3-9 Doors on cabinets with faceframes may be lipped, flush or overlaid.

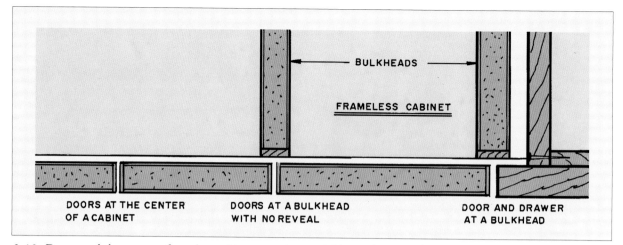

BULKHEADS

FRAMELESS CABINET

DOORS AT THE CENTER OF A CABINET   DOORS AT A BULKHEAD WITH NO REVEAL   DOOR AND DRAWER AT A BULKHEAD

3-10 Doors and drawers on frameless cabinets are the overlaid type because they must cover the edges of the carcass, as seen in this view from above of the construction.

OVERLAID DOORS

Overlaid doors overhang the faceframe and so, if something is off—out of square—just a little, the door will still close against the faceframe. Overlaid doors are widely used on both faceframe and frameless cabinets. Details for frameless cabinets are shown in **3-10**. Simple overlaid doors made from particleboard that were sealed, primed, and painted are shown in **3-11**.

3-11 Simple overlaid doors have been made from flat particleboard panels that were sealed, primed, and painted.

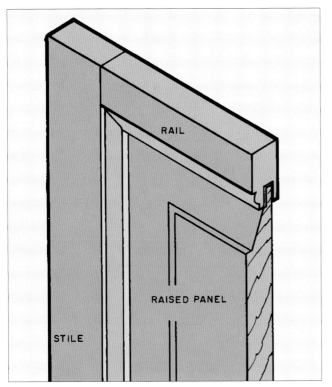

3-13 Typical construction of a cabinet door with a solid-wood raised panel.

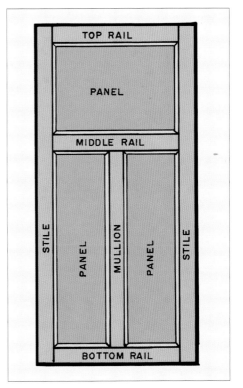

3-12 The construction and terminology used for a raised-panel doorframe.

RAISED-PANEL
DOORS

Raised-panel doors are widely used on kitchen cabinets and bath vanities. The door has a frame of solid wood composed of stiles, rails, and sometimes a mullion (**3-12**). The panels are usually solid-wood strips edge-glued and machined as desired (**3-13**). A finished raised-panel door is in **3-14**. In **3-14** the doors meet on a mullion. However, they could be installed without the mullion, leaving only a small space between them.

3-14 These raised-panel doors are separated by a mullion that is part of the faceframe.

When the doors are closed, a mullion appears to cover the space between them.

When the doors open, the mullion swings with one of the doors, providing a wide opening for sliding shelves to move easily out of the cabinet.

Some people, when choosing their cabinets, do not like to leave this gap, so they install a thin piece of wood to the back of one door, covering the space, as shown in **3-15**. This solution to the noticeable gap does have the disadvantage that when you open the door with the strip you force open the adjoining door. The raised panel could be made from medium density fiberboard (MDF) with a hardwood veneer or plastic laminate bonded to it. Another type has the raised panel molded from MDF and finished with a polyvinyl (PVC) coating, which is then painted.

DRAWERS

Drawers are constructed to be used on cabinets with faceframes and frameless units in the same manner as described for doors. Drawers on frameless cabinets are overlaid as shown for doors in **3-16**. With faceframes they may be lipped, flush, or overlaid, as shown in **3-17**.

3-15 (Top and left) If doors meet without a mullion and you do not want a crack to be visible, a thin wood strip is fastened to the inside of one of the doors. This permits the use of slidng shelves, as shown in 3-40.

CONSTRUCTING KITCHENS

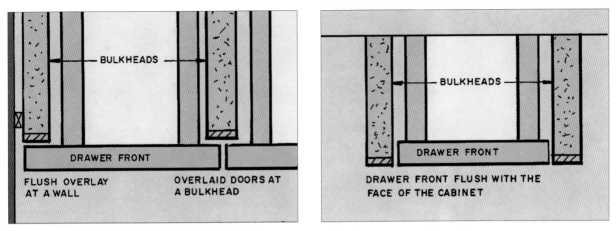

BULKHEADS

DRAWER FRONT

FLUSH OVERLAY
AT A WALL

OVERLAID DOORS AT
A BULKHEAD

BULKHEADS

DRAWER FRONT

DRAWER FRONT FLUSH WITH THE
FACE OF THE CABINET

3-16 Typical drawer-front assemblies for cabinets without a faceframe, as seen from above.

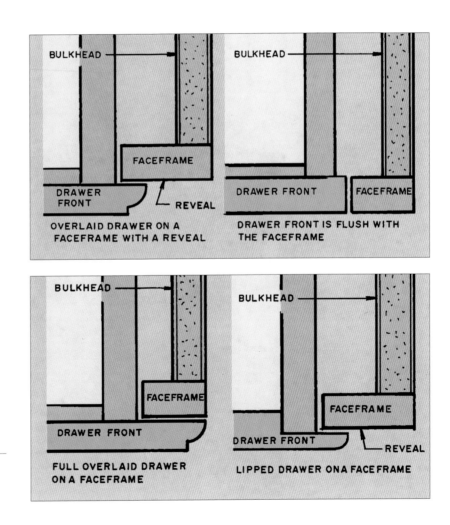

BULKHEAD

FACEFRAME

DRAWER
FRONT

REVEAL

OVERLAID DRAWER ON A
FACEFRAME WITH A REVEAL

BULKHEAD

DRAWER FRONT

FACEFRAME

DRAWER FRONT IS FLUSH WITH
THE FACEFRAME

BULKHEAD

FACEFRAME

DRAWER FRONT

FULL OVERLAID DRAWER
ON A FACEFRAME

BULKHEAD

FACEFRAME

DRAWER FRONT

REVEAL

LIPPED DRAWER ON A FACEFRAME

3-17 Typical drawer front assemblies for cabinets with a faceframe, as seen from above.

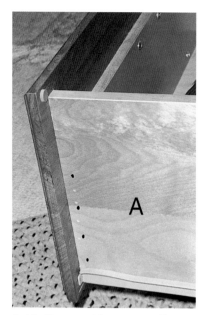
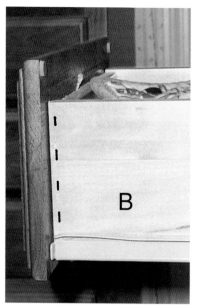
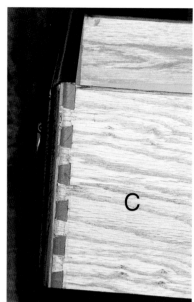

3-18 Drawer sides are usually secured to the drawer front with dovetails, nails, staples, or screws. Drawer A has nails, B staples, and C is dovetailed.

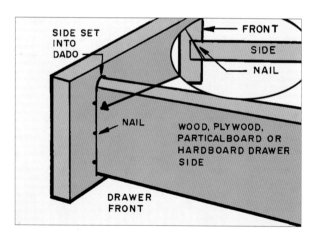
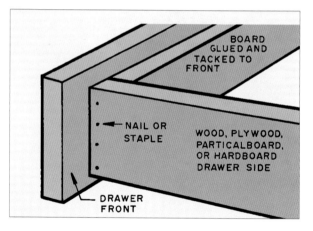
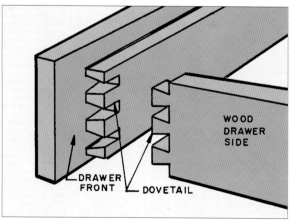

3-19 Typical dovetail- and mechanically joined drawerfront connections.

SIDES OF DRAWERS

Drawer sides may be hardwood, particleboard, or hardboard, while bottoms may be hardboard or plywood. The drawer sides are connected to the drawer front with dovetails or stapled, nailed, or secured with screws (**3-18**). The joints are also glued. Each of these if properly made produces drawers that will last many years. The dovetail joint is more expensive and is used in higher-quality cabinets (**3-19**).

INSTALLING DRAWER GLIDES

For the most efficient use of kitchen drawers, it is recommended that the cabinet drawers be installed with steel glides with nylon rollers, such as those in **3-20** and **3-21**. These move the drawer easily and quietly. The use of a single drawer guide down the center of a drawer does not produce the results desired, especially if the drawer carries relatively heavy items.

3-20 This bottom-mounted drawer glide is used on small drawers that will carry light loads.

3-21 This large heavy-duty drawer glide will move large drawers with heavy loads smoothly and easily.

SHELVES

Shelves are made from ⅜- to ¾-inch plywood or particleboard. The longer the span, the thicker the material to be used. Shelves that are too thin will eventually sag. The Kitchen Cabinet Manufacturers Association has standard tests to check the strength of shelves.

Shelves in base cabinets are often fixed, whereas shelves in wall cabinets are usually made to be adjustable. They typically use some type of metal or plastic clip that fits into holes drilled in the side of the cabinet (3-22). Some high-quality cabinets use metal shelf standards for adjustable shelves (3-23).

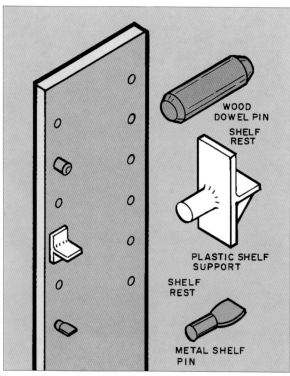

WOOD DOWEL PIN

SHELF REST

PLASTIC SHELF SUPPORT

SHELF REST

METAL SHELF PIN

3-22 Shelf pins are widely used to provide support for adjustable shelves.

3-23 Metal shelf standards provide an excellent way to support adjustable shelves.

CARCASS MATERIALS

Carcass materials are typically either plywood or particleboard. Plywood carcasses on the exposed ends of cabinets can be made using sheets having the desired veneer bonded as the sheet was made. Particleboard end panels (bulkheads) have a **vinyl** or **paper film** having a wood-grain image or a solid color bonded to them. These are low cost and not as durable as other laminates. Another laminate is a paper layer saturated with a **melamine resin**. This material is a **low-pressure laminate**. It is more durable than the paper film laminate. **High-pressure laminates** are the best for use on exterior surfaces where they are likely to be damaged. This product is made by bonding multiple layers of resin-impregnated paper fused together under heat and pressure to form a hard, durable sheet. On cabinets where this is used the lower-pressure laminate is often used on the interior surfaces of the cabinet.

HARDWARE

A widely used hinge is one that is completely concealed. In **3-24** is a series of concealed hinges used on frameless European-style cabinets. One side of the hinge is set in a recess that is cut in the door.

Courtesy Julius Blum, Inc.

100° Swing

125° Swing

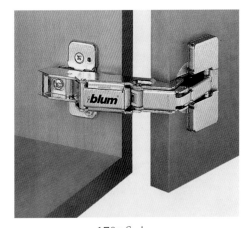

170° Swing

3-24 Three of the concealed hinges providing control over the opening angle of the door. These are used on frameless cabinets.

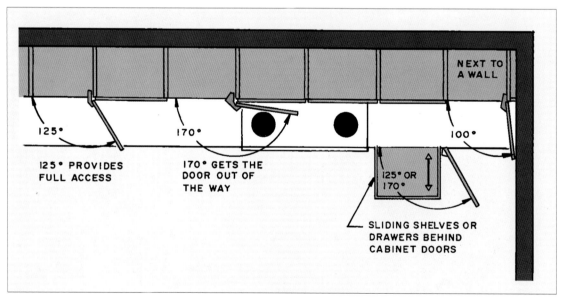

SHELF

BULKHEAD

DOOR

100°

170°

125°

110°

Courtesy Julius Blum, Inc.

NEXT TO A WALL

125°

170°

100°

125° PROVIDES FULL ACCESS

170° GETS THE DOOR OUT OF THE WAY

125° OR 170°

SLIDING SHELVES OR DRAWERS BEHIND CABINET DOORS

3-26 When selecting hinges be aware of possible problems caused by their location.

The selection of concealed hinges are made to allow the door to open a specified number of degrees, as shown in **3-25**. When you design your cabinets, select the hinge that permits the door to open as needed to access the cabinet interior yet not swing open too far and strike and damage cabinets or a wall beside it. Applications are shown in **3-26**. It is important when cabinets have shelves that slide out that the door opens enough to let them operate without interference from the door.

When you have a cabinet on a diagonal, concealed diagonal hinges can be used (**3-27**). They are available for a wide range of angles and for overlay and inset doors.

These hinges have adjusting screws permitting you to reposition the door some after the hinges have been installed. The door can be removed from the cabinet by lifting the top of the long leaf secured to a plate inside the cabinet (**3-28**).

3-27 This angled hinge is used on cabinets having the front of the cabinet on an angle to the adjoining cabinets.

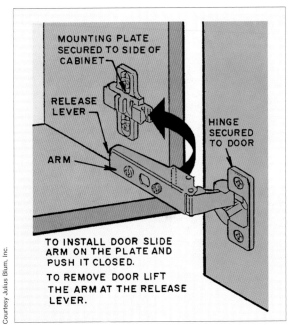

3-28 This hinge permits the door to be removed and replaced by simply moving the arm.

A concealed hinge for use on cabinets with a faceframe is shown in **3-29**. Again the hinge is set in a recess in the door and secured to the faceframe inside the cabinet.

There are a wide variety of hinges that are decorative and designed to be visible on the front of the cabinet. A few are shown in **3-30**.

Another kind of useful hinge is the semi-concealed hinge such as the barrel hinge shown in **3-31**. These are widely used on stock cabinets. Notice the screws are in slotted openings, allowing a little adjustment for straightening the door. The barrel is visible and adds a decorative feature. The barrel hinge is a self-closing hinge that holds the door closed so a cabinet door catch is not needed.

3-29 This is a compact concealed hinge used on cabinets with a faceframe.

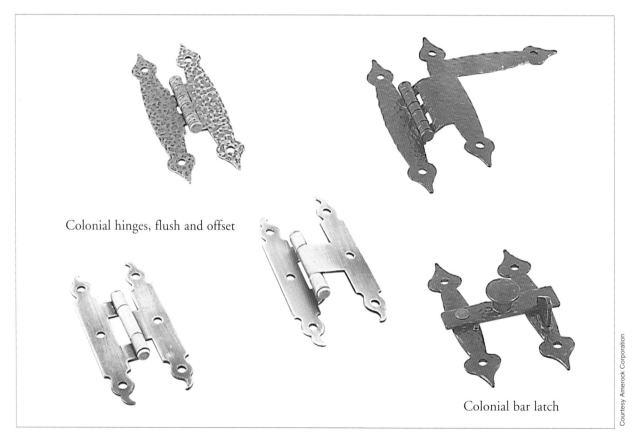

Colonial hinges, flush and offset

Colonial bar latch

3-30 These hinges are decorative and surface-mounted and add to the style of the cabinet.

3-31 The barrel hinge is a semiconcealed hinge. It exposes only the barrel, which is decorative. The hinge in "A" is a self-closing hinge so no door catch is required. The hinge in "B" is a large, decorative hinge and is used with a magnetic door catch.

Hinge "A" is a semiconcealed, self-closing hinge.

Hinge "B" is a semiconcealed, decorative, long-barreled hinge.

The various **drawer** and **door handles** chosen must complement the design and color of the cabinets. Some popular types are in **3-32**. Other classical styles that enhance the overall appearance of your cabinets are in **3-33**, **3-34**, and **3-35**.

One solution to providing a way to open a door or drawer is with a shaped wood strip that provides a finger-gripping recess. These are solid wood and are bonded to the bottom edge of a door or drawer front (**3-36**).

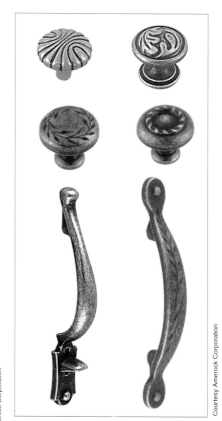

3-33 Wrought-iron hardware gives a dark, textured appearance and works well with light- and dark-colored cabinet woods.

Courtesy Amerock Corporation

3-32 Some of the drawer and door handles available.

CONSTRUCTING KITCHENS

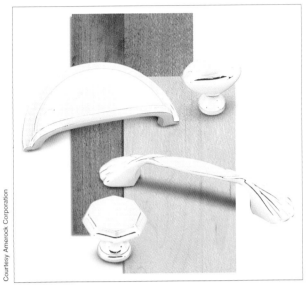

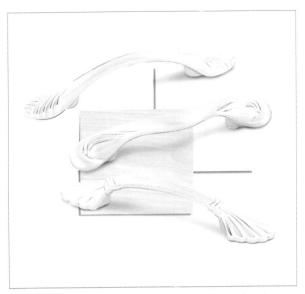

3-34 Solid-brass hardware adds a warmth and richness to the kitchen and can be used on any cabinet finish.

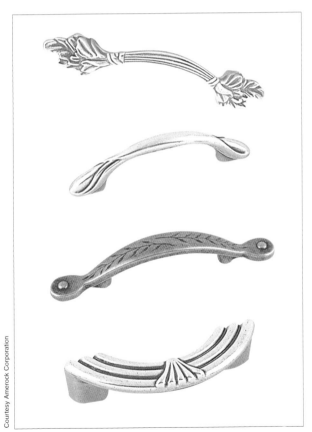

3-35 (Above and middle right) Burnished-brass hardware has a darker but reflective finish that is suitable for use on light and dark cabinetry.

3-36 This shaped wood strip on the bottom of a door or top of a drawer front provides the means to grip and open it.

Courtesy G.E. Appliances

3-37 These sliding wire basket drawers provide storage for fruits and vegetables.

3-38 Wall-hung wire shelves can store items frequently used during meal preparation.

CONSTRUCTING KITCHENS

3-39 There are a wide variety of wire racks you can place inside the cabinets to increase the storage capacity.

OTHER STORAGE FEATURES

Cabinet manufacturers offer a wide range of accessories. Many can be bought at building supply dealers and added to your cabinets whenever you decide you can use them.

Many types of wire carrier are available. They are installed to increase the storage capacity of a cabinet. A few of those available are shown in **3-37**, **3-38**, and **3-39**.

Another very valuable storage option is the use of sliding shelves. These can be installed in wall and base cabinets (**3-40**), tall cabinets, and pantries (**3-41**). Shallow sliding drawers in tall cabinets are especially useful (**3-42**).

Two approaches to increasing the utilization of the space under the counter are shown in **3-43** and **3-44**. One uses a series of drawers of varying depths. The top shallow drawers can hold silver, spices, and other small items. Large things as cereal boxes or paper towel rolls can be stored in the larger drawers.

3-40 This base cabinet has sliding drawer/shelves which make the rear of the shelf easily accessible.

3-41 This tall cabinet has a series of wire framed pull-out shelves and storage on the inside of the door.

3-42 This tall cabinet conceals a bank of interior roll-out trays and a pull-out surround with bottle storage on the bottom.

3-43 This multidrawer unit provides several drawers of different depths. It is compatible with the 32mm system.

3-44 This is a three-drawer base storage unit that has a single front covering the drawers, providing the appearance of a door.

A drawer system providing two large deep drawers is shown in **3-45**. After the cabinetmaker makes the wood back, bottom, and front, the hardware provided fits into holes that have been drilled in the pieces. The hardware in the predrilled holes holds the drawer together. The metal sides also serve as the drawer glides.

Manufacturers produce a vast array of other storage products. In **3-46** is a wine rack built to standard base-cabinet size. It has a cooling unit to keep the wine at the recommended temperature. Notice other features such as the china display cabinet, spice drawers below it, and display shelves below the wall cabinet.

Courtesy Julius Blum, Inc.

3-45 This drawer has wood back, front, and bottom and is held together by manufacturer-supplied connections and metal sides.

CABINET DOOR CATCHES

Many manufactured cabinets do not have door catches. They use self-closing hinges as shown earlier in **3-30**. If catches are used, magnetic types are recommended. The others, spring and roller types, do not give the easy operation available with magnetic catches. These are shown in **3-47**.

Courtesy Sub-Zero Freezer Co., Inc.

3-46 This kitchen has a wine storage unit designed to fit in with the standard base cabinet.

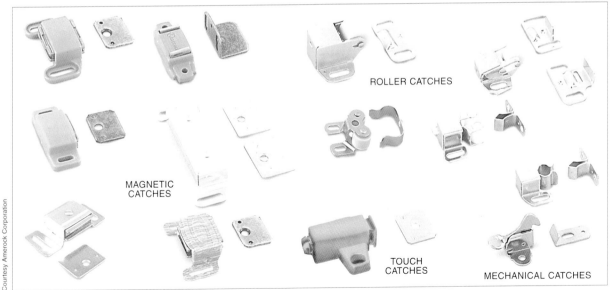

ROLLER CATCHES

MAGNETIC CATCHES

TOUCH CATCHES

MECHANICAL CATCHES

Courtesy Amerock Corporation

3-47 These are the most commonly used cabinet door catches.

COUNTERTOPS

Granite is much harder than marble and is less likely to chip or stain. Typically ¾ inch thick, this is very expensive and requires considerable preliminary planning so the pieces can be cut and polished by the supplier before being shipped to your kitchen.

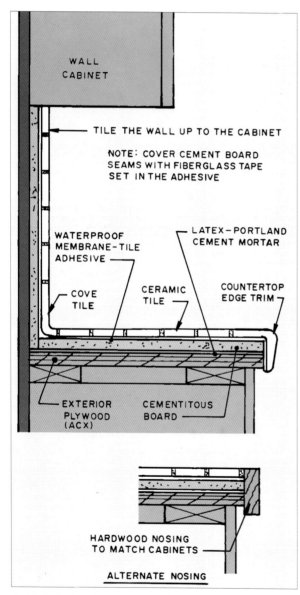

3-48 Tile should be set on a base of cement board or a bed of mortar.

Marble, like granite, is expensive and requires cutting by professional marble cutters. It is subject to staining and chipping.

Ceramic tile countertops are hard, tough, and resistant to damage from heat. The major problem with tile countertops is the grout. It is a cement mix and will stain, crack, and mildew. Better grouts are being developed. An epoxy grout is being used successfully. It sets hard yet is somewhat flexible, thus reducing cracking. It also is stain resistant. While it costs more than cement-type grouts, it is an expense that should be given favorable consideration.

Most people favor a matte finish on ceramic tile. The gloss finish tends to scratch.

You can install a wood edge on the countertop and lay the tile to it, or use a tile nosing (3-48).

While tile can be bonded directly to a plywood or particleboard substrate, this is not recommended. The grout between the tiles does deteriorate and will let moisture get below the tiles, causing failure. The tile should be set on cement board or a bed of mortar as shown in 3-48. Generally the tile is placed on the wall up to the bottom of the wall cabinets. A wide variety of colors, patterns, and sizes are available (3-49).

3-49 Ceramic tile is available in a wide variety of colors. Glazed tiles are easiest to clean. Matte-finished tiles hide scratches better than glass tiles.

High-pressure plastic laminates are the most widely used counter-top surfacing material. This material consists of several layers of kraft paper impregnated with phenolic resins and a layer of translucent colored or printed paper treated with a melamine resin on top. These are then placed under heat and pressure, forming a sheet about 1/16 inch thick.

High-pressure plastic laminates are not affected by water, but will scratch if hit by something sharp. You will not want to cut foods on this kind of surface; use a cutting board. They will also scorch when exposed to excessive heat. A wide variety of colors and patterns are available. These will vary depending upon the manufacturer (**3-50**). Plastic laminates will stain but clean easily. A matte finish will not scratch as easily as a gloss finish, and scratches will not be as apparent when they occur.

Courtesy Formica Corporation

3-50 Several popular colors and patterns of high-pressure plastic laminates used on kitchen countertops.

3-51 This countertop has high-pressure plastic laminate bonded to the substrate and the edge of the top banded with wood that matches the cabinets.

High-pressure plastic laminates are bonded to industrial-grade particleboard or plywood at least ¾ inches thick. The sheets can be installed on the substrate, butting a wood edge (3-51) or by bonding a piece of laminate to the edge. If you use this technique you will have a dark edge showing where the laminate has been trimmed flush with the top. Notice the wall above the backsplash has been tiled.

Postformed laminate tops have a continuous sheet of laminate formed over the front edge and running to the wall up over the backsplash (3-52). A detail drawing is in 3-53.

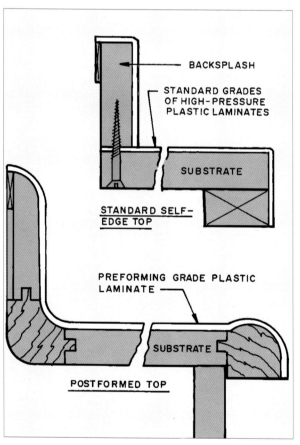

3-53 A typical detail showing the substrate built for postformed high-pressure plastic laminate countertops compared with standard laminated tops.

3-52 This postformed high-pressure plastic laminate has continuous coverage from the rounded edge to the top of the backsplash.

Usually the wall above the backsplash on plastic laminate countertops is tiled up to the wall cabinet (**3-54**).

Solid-surface countertop materials are a cast plastic resin such as acrylic, polyester, or a combination of them and mineral fillers. They have the advantage of having the color completely through the material. They are waterproof and resist stains, heat, and scratches. However, take care and do not abuse them. Some types have a special compound you can use to repair chips. Minor scratches can be buffed or lightly sanded out because the color goes all the way through the material. They are available in a variety of solid colors, granitelike materials, and patterns. Solid-surface countertop materials are more expensive than high-pressure plastic laminates.

One such product is the Swanstone® molded solid-surface countertop shown in **3-55**. This seamless molded-edge countertop is sold in lengths and is cut and installed with existing tools. It is impact resistant, resists damage from heat and cold, and cleans with normal detergent. Scratches can be buffed out with a fine steel-

Courtesy The Swan Corporation

3-55 This is a molded, seamless, solid-surface countertop. It is durable and easy to clean.

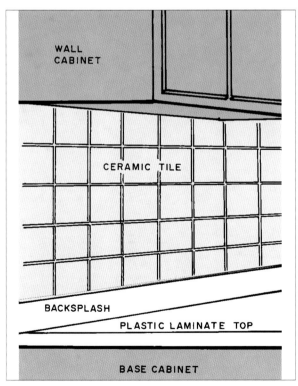

WALL CABINET

CERAMIC TILE

BACKSPLASH

PLASTIC LAMINATE TOP

BASE CABINET

3-54 Ceramic tile is often laid on the wall above the backsplash of plastic laminate and solid-surface countertops.

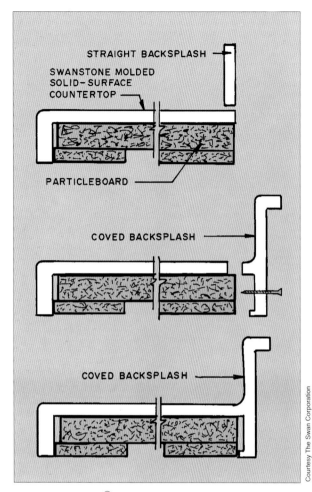

3-56 Swanstone® solid-surface countertops have several ways to build the backsplash.

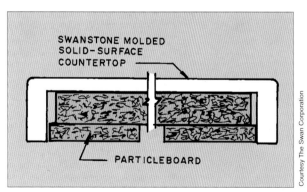

3-57 This Swanstone® countertop is used on island and peninsula counters.

wool or abrasive paper. It is available with a splashback bonded to the wall or a molded coved splashback as shown in **3-56**. It is also made with molded edges for use on islands and peninsulas (**3-57**). A finished installation with a drop-in top mounted sink is in **3-58**. Sinks made from Swanstone® can be top or undermounted as shown in **3-59**. More details on these and other sinks is in Chapter 7.

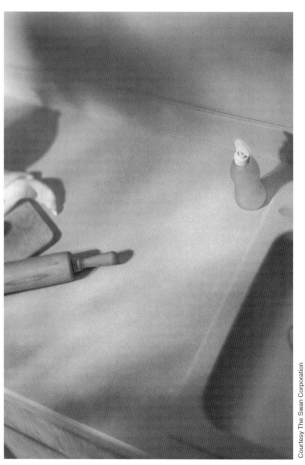

3-58 A Swanstone® countertop with a drop-in sink of the same color material.

Another solid surfacing material that you might want to consider using is a product called Surell® that is manufactured by Formica Corporation. This is a solid, dense resin and mineral composite that has a smooth outer finish. It has a range of colors and patterns. One example is in **3-60**. The colors and pattern run all the way through the material. A lighter countertop can be seen in **3-61**.

3-60 This solid surfacing material gives the appearance of stone.

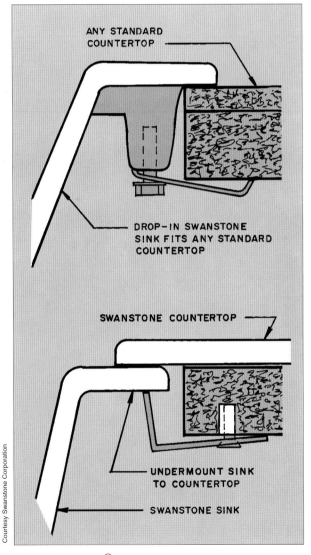

3-59 Swanstone® sinks are available for drop-in and undermount installations.

3-61 The light color Surell® solid-surface countertop blends with the color of the cabinets.

Avonite® is another solid surfacing material used on countertops, furniture, wall cladding, and other interior design and architectural applications where a waterproof and durable material is needed. Avonite® is a patented composite nonporous material that has a uniform color throughout its entire thickness. It is available in either polyester or acrylic. It is formed into sinks as shown in **3-61**.

Another material used for sinks and countertops is referred to as **cultured marble**. It has a thin gel-coat surface and is too soft to withstand the heavy use that occurs in a kitchen. The bathroom sink and countertop in **3-62** is made from cultured marble. It consists of marble chips and dust cast into a polyester resin. More expensive sinks and countertops have a thicker gel-coat which helps resist crazing and cracking.

Courtesy Avonite, Inc.

3-61 This countertop and sink is formed from Avonite®, a solid surfacing material that finds many uses on architectural products.

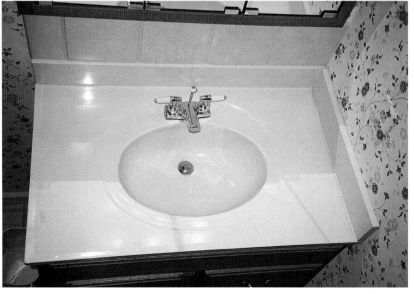

3-62 This bath lavatory and countertop is molded from cultured marble. There are no seams.

Stainless-steel countertops are usually associated with restaurant and hospital installations. If there is a fabricator you can contact, you can have excellent countertops custom-made for your kitchen. Stainless-steel countertops are waterproof, will not stain, are easy to clean, and resist damage from heat. If you opt for this material, get a gauge thick enough so that it will not dent easily. Seams will have to be welded, ground smooth, and polished. Your stainless-steel sink can be welded to the countertop, making a watertight seal (**3-63**).

3-63 Stainless-steel sinks can have long drainboards and even cover the entire top of the cabinet.

CHAPTER 4

Kitchen Layout

Before you can begin to make the actual kitchen layout you will need to gather some information. **First**, make a simple drawing of the kitchen and record all dimensions. **Second**, you will need to decide the types and brands of appliances. Get actual sizes from your local dealer. **Third**, select the brand of cabinets to be used and get the sizes that are available from the dealer.

For a new house under construction, you cannot finalize your layout until the kitchen is actually finished with wall material and casing around doors and windows (4-1). While you can make a preliminary layout from the architect's drawing, the finished size can vary. If this is a remodeling job, you can measure the room after any wall and casing replacements have been made.

There are a number of ways to get to the final kitchen plan. The following covers suggestions to do this. Begin by making a **preliminary drawing** upon which you will record the actual room dimensions (4-2). The scale "½ inch equals one foot" is a good size to use. If you have access to an architect's scale it will have one scale marked ½. The end of this scale is marked into units representing ½-inch divisions (4-3). The rest of the scale is divided into feet.

Draw the room to scale, locating doors and windows. Measure over the casing, as shown in 4-2. Record the measurements in inches. On the plan indicate windows and doors using the symbols shown in 4-4. Note the swing of doors just in case it may cause interference with some part of a cabinet or appliance.

Courtesy Formica Corporation

4-1 Locating the sink near a source of outdoor light is desirable. Be sure to note the measurements for any window or door casings as you are preparing your preliminary drawing.

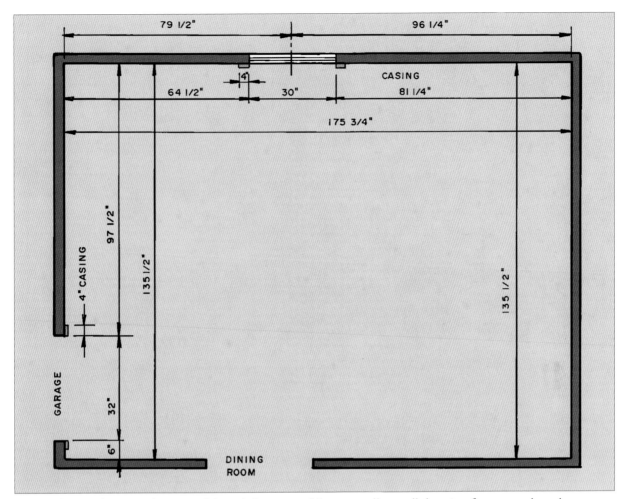

4-2 Make a preliminary drawing of the existing room. Measure wall to wall, locating features such as doors, windows, and the casings around them. If it is a complete remodeling job, locate the existing plumbing, electrical outlets, and lights. This gives the information needed for making an accurate scale drawing.

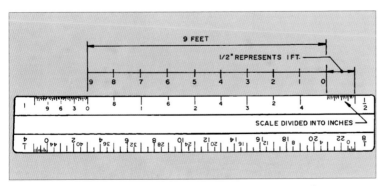

4-3 An architect's scale allows you to let a chosen unit of measurement represent one foot on your drawing, such as ½ inch = 1 foot.

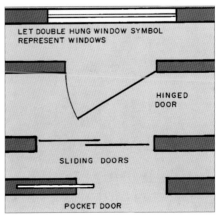

4-4 Frequently used door and window symbols.

Measure as carefully and accurately as you can. A small error could make it possible that the row of cabinets and appliances is too long and one or more cabinets may have to be replaced. Actually, if the cabinets are a little short, filler strips are available from the cabinet manufacturer to fill any gap between cabinets or between cabinets and a wall.

Since you know the size of your appliances, the sizes of cabinets available, and the size of the room, it is now time to consult the principles for planning a kitchen and using them to begin locating the major work centers as described in Chapter 1.

Now you can begin to plan the kitchen layout. Using the dimensions on the preliminary drawing, make an accurate scale drawing of the room, such as shown in 4-5. You could use graph paper with ¼-inch squares; at the scale of ½ inch equals 1 foot, each square represents 6 inches.

Now let's see how to proceed. One way to quickly construct a variety of trial layouts is to make scale cardboard templates of the appliances, place them on the floor plan, and measure distances to walls, doors, windows, and other cabinets. Check the work triangle and move appliances to see if you can improve the efficiency of the kitchen. Check it against the planning

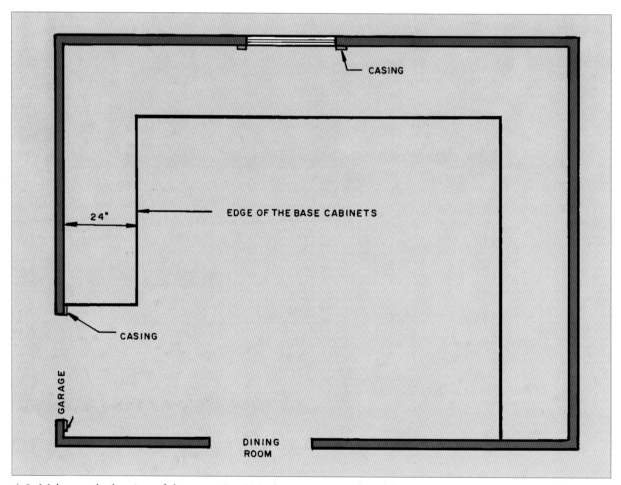

4-5 Make a scale drawing of the room. Let ½ inch represent one lineal foot. Locate the edge of the base cabinets on the plan.

CONSTRUCTING KITCHENS

principles. As you work you will begin to fix the location of the work centers. Once you feel you have them in the best place, you can turn your attention to the base cabinets.

Plan the location of the appliances and base cabinets next. Wait to figure the wall cabinets until after the appliances and base cabinet decisions have been made.

Draw the edge of the base cabinet along the walls in the same way as seen in 4-4. Most base cabinets are 24 inches wide. Now place the appliances in various locations on the plan and check as to how the planning principles (in Chapter 1) relate to your possible solution. One trial solution with comments is given in 4-6. A **U-shaped** kitchen was selected with cabinets chosen from the standard sizes listed in Chapter 3, and using the following appliances:

Refrigerator	30 inches wide
Dishwasher	24 inches wide
Compactor	15 inches wide
Double bowl sink	36-inch wide cabinet
Surface cooking unit	30 inches wide
Wall oven	30 inches wide

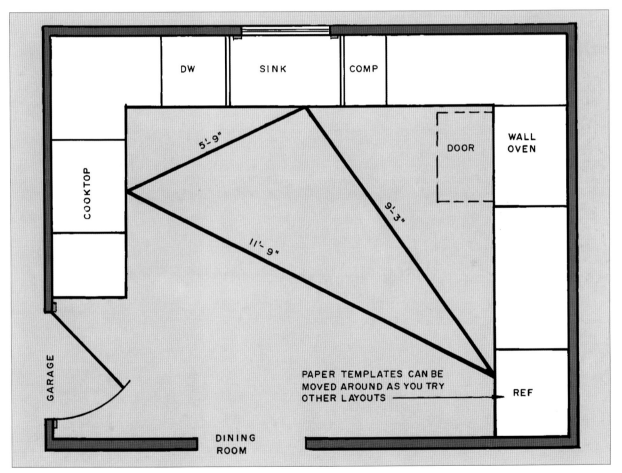

4-6 This trial layout has a number of problems. The work triangle is 26'-9", which is the maximum recommended. The refrigerator is away from the garage door, making storage of frozen and cold storage items a little more difficult. It is also away from the door to the dining room, making a long walk to serve cold foods from it. The wall oven creates a dead corner in the countertop. The countertop space for food preparation is limited. The oven door blocks the side countertop.

Continue to move appliances and check the planning principles until you reach a satisfactory solution. The solution shown in 4-7 is a possible adequate layout. The sink was located under the window and serves as the center of the cleanup area. The dishwasher and compactor were located beside the sink to complete the cleanup area. This long wall provides adequate counterspace. The refrigerator was placed at the end of the counter to the left of the sink—it is next to the door from the garage through which the food will enter the kitchen. It is also convenient for serving the dining room. The countertop beside it will serve as a preparation area. Remember to buy a refrigerator

with a door that is hinged on the left side. The cooktop is to the right of the sink. Here is adequate countertop for cleanup and food preparation for cooking and baking. The work triangle is within recommended limits. All appliance doors are free of any obstructions. A small dining area has been made available.

Now that you have located the appliances you can start choosing and sizing the base cabinets. For example, in one place you may want a unit entirely of drawers and elsewhere one with a drawer and door or just full doors. Also consider special cabinets such as those with sliding shelves and wire racks for special storage jobs.

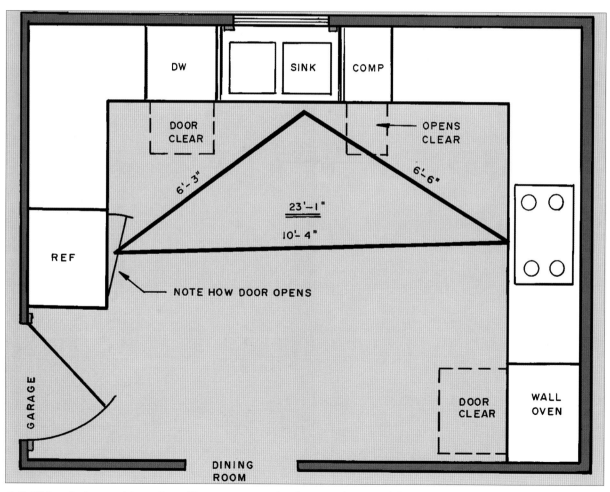

4-7 This solution positions the refrigerator nearer the doors and moves the oven into a less useful corner. A large preparation counter is provided and the work triangle has been shortened.

CONSTRUCTING KITCHENS

SELECT CABINET SIZES & TYPES

Begin selecting sizes of base cabinets by starting on the wall with a window. Work to the left and right from the centerline. As you move in each direction subtract the width of the cabinet from the available distance. This kitchen has 55 inches to the left of the sink for base cabinets and appliances (4-8). The sink cabinet and dishwasher took most of the space. Room for a lazy Susan corner cabinet was available and a 1½-inch space was left and was filled with a filler strip.

Cabinets are identified on the drawing using a series of letters and numbers. These were developed by the National Kitchen and Bath Association. Most manufacturers use these and in some cases have developed symbols for cabinets that they make that are unique.

The **first letter** indicates the general type of cabinet, such as **W**—wall cabinet or **B**—base cabinet. The **second letter** (when used) gives more specific information, such as **WC**—wall corner cabinet or **BC**—base corner cabinet. **Wall symbols** are followed by **four numbers**. The first two give the width of the cabinet and the last two the height, as in **W3630**. This cabinet is 36 inches wide and 30 inches high. **Base cabinet letter codes** are followed by **two numbers** giving the width of the cabinet as **B36** which is 36 inches wide. Letters may follow the numbers to give additional information that is unusual—**WC-D** would identify a corner wall cabinet that is on a diagonal; **BC-LS** is a corner base cabinet with a lazy Susan.

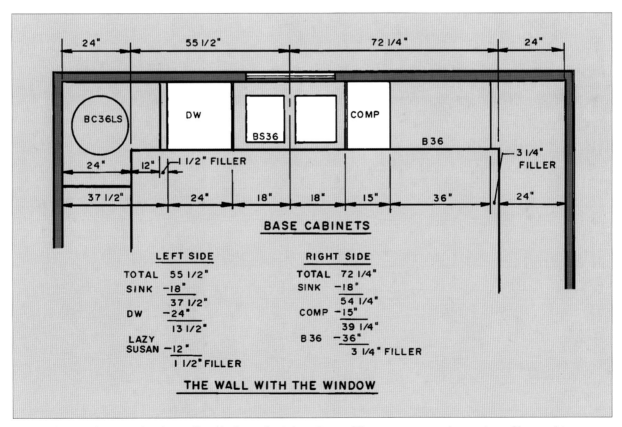

4-8 Cabinet selections for the wall with the sink. A lazy Susan fills one corner and a section of base cabinet butts the base cabinet on the right wall. Several filler strips are needed.

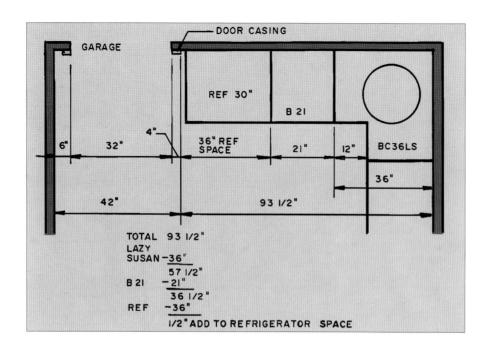

GARAGE

DOOR CASING

REF 30"

B 21

36" REF SPACE

BC36LS

6"　32"　4"　　36"　21"　12"

36"

42"　　　　93 1/2"

TOTAL　93 1/2"
LAZY
SUSAN ‐36"
　　　 57 1/2"
B 21　‐21"
　　　 36 1/2"
REF　‐36"
1/2" ADD TO REFRIGERATOR SPACE

4-9 The wall with the door to the garage puts a base cabinet between the refrigerator and the lazy Susan cabinet in the corner. The space for the refrigerator was 36 inches even though a 30-inch unit was planned. This allows for installation of a larger refrigerator at some future time.

The most frequently used symbols for cabinets are given in **Table 4-1**, as developed by the National Kitchen and Bath Association.

In **4-9** is a layout for the wall with the door from the garage. Wall space for base cabinets is 93½ inches, which is clear of the casing around the door. This base meets the lazy Susan corner cabinet, which requires 12 inches on the front of the counter. The total corner unit is 36 inches wide. A 21-inch base cabinet was placed next, leaving 36 inches clear for a refrigerator. Most refrigerators are narrower than this, so the spacing is adequate for the common sizes of residential refrigerators.

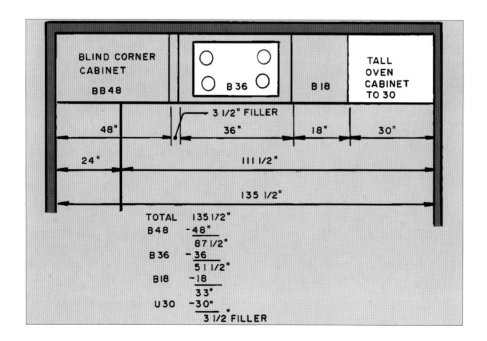

BLIND CORNER CABINET
BB48

B 36

B 18

TALL OVEN CABINET TO 30

3 1/2" FILLER

48"　36"　18"　30"

24"　　111 1/2"

135 1/2"

TOTAL　135 1/2"
B48　‐48"
　　　 87 1/2"
B 36　‐36
　　　 51 1/2"
B18　‐18
　　　 33"
U30　‐30"
　　　 3 1/2 FILLER

4-10 This wall of cabinets uses a tall oven utility cabinet in the corner, which makes the space very useful.

TABLE 4-1 SYMBOLS FOR CABINETS

BASE CABINET IDENTIFICATION

B	Base cabinet
BS	Base sink
BD	Base all drawers
BSC	Base sink corner diagonal
BSF	Base sink front
TO	Tall oven cabinet
TU	Tall utility cabinet
BC-LS	Base corner, lazy Susan
BC	Base corner
BB	Base blank corner
B-ROS	Base roll-out trays
BP	Base peninsula

WALL CABINET IDENTIFICATION

W	Wall cabinet
WP	Peninsula wall cabinet
WB	Wall cabinet, blank corner
WC-D	Wall cabinet, corner diagonal
WC	Wall corner cabinet
WBC	Wall blank corner
WM	Wall microwave
WC-PC	90° wall corner

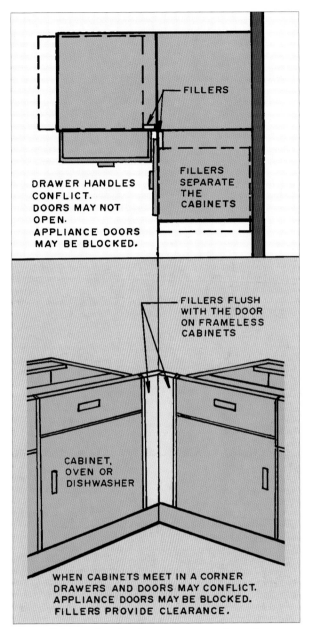

DRAWER HANDLES CONFLICT. DOORS MAY NOT OPEN. APPLIANCE DOORS MAY BE BLOCKED.

FILLERS

FILLERS SEPARATE THE CABINETS

FILLERS FLUSH WITH THE DOOR ON FRAMELESS CABINETS

CABINET, OVEN OR DISHWASHER

WHEN CABINETS MEET IN A CORNER DRAWERS AND DOORS MAY CONFLICT. APPLIANCE DOORS MAY BE BLOCKED. FILLERS PROVIDE CLEARANCE.

4-11 Cabinets butting in a corner may have drawers and doors that conflict when you try to open them. Space them apart with fillers. Frameless cabinets are used in this example.

In **4-10** is the layout for the other wall. The total room width is 135½ inches. A blind corner unit 48 inches long was used. After adding the cooktop base, an 18-inch drawer base, and a wall oven cabinet, 3½ inches were left. This can be taken care of with one or more filler strips between cabinets or the cabinet and the wall.

WATCHING FOR CONFLICTS

As you select and place cabinets be certain to check for conflicts between drawers, doors, doors and drawers, or doors and walls. Some common conflicts are shown in **4-11** above, and **4-12** and

4-13 on the next page. These conflicts can be relieved by using fillers. Fillers are 3-inch-wide strips available from the cabinet manufacturer and are finished to match the cabinets. They space the cabinets, providing the needed clearance. This is more of a problem if you are using frameless cabinets. Many cabinets with faceframes have adequate clearance for most applications.

Fillers on cabinets with faceframes are placed so they are flush with the faceframe (4-14). If the cabinets are frameless the fillers are lined up with the door as shown in **4-15**.

LAYING OUT THE WALL CABINETS

After the base cabinets have been set, locate the wall cabinets. Draw a line on the floor plan 12 inches from the wall to represent the edge of the wall cabinets. These are planned much like the

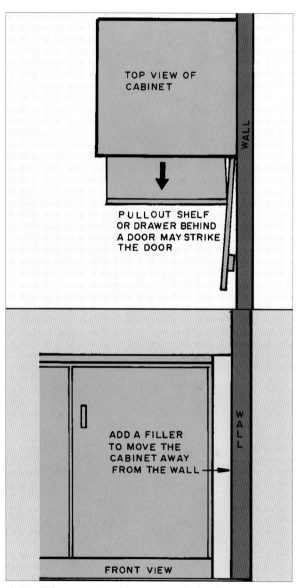

4-12 When a cabinet butts a wall, the door may not open wide enough to allow pull-out shelves and drawers to open fully. A filler at the wall will enable the door to swing back out of the way.

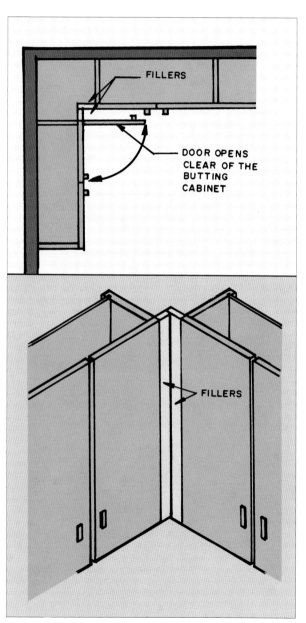

4-13 Be certain to check the wall cabinets for conflicts in the same manner as the base cabinets.

CONSTRUCTING KITCHENS

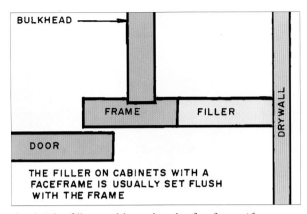

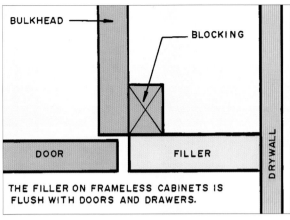

4-14 The filler could overlay the faceframe if you like the recessed appearance.Usually it is set flush, as shown, on cabinets with a faceframe.

4-15 On cabinets without a faceframe the filler is set against blocking, flush with the door or drawers.

base cabinets. Work from each side of the appliances after you decide on the cabinet to be above them. The range will have a hood of some type and will be the center point of the cabinets on that wall. Cabinets over the refrigerator must clear the refrigerator, leaving an airspace of several inches on each side.

The wall cabinets should be lined up with the base cabinets and appliances as much as possible. In 4-16 they begin beside the window casing and can clear it an inch or two as necessary to get the widths to fit along the wall. Notice the wall cabinet size is indicated by a symbol such as W3630. This means "wall cabinet 36 inches

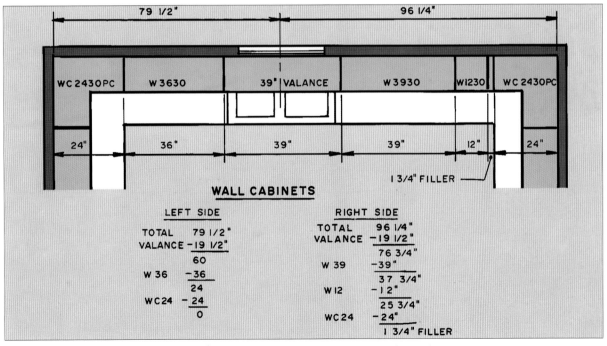

4-16 Wall cabinets are laid out after the base cabinets and appliances are located.

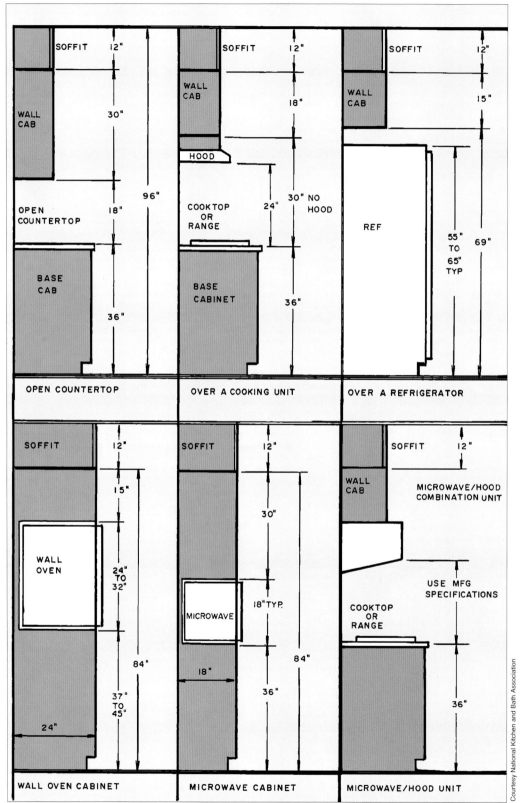

SOFFIT 12"

WALL CAB 30"

OPEN COUNTERTOP 18"

BASE CAB 36"

96"

OPEN COUNTERTOP

SOFFIT 12"

WALL CAB 18"

HOOD

COOKTOP OR RANGE 24"

BASE CABINET 36"

30" NO HOOD

OVER A COOKING UNIT

SOFFIT 12"

WALL CAB 15"

REF

55" TO 65" TYP 69"

OVER A REFRIGERATOR

SOFFIT 12"

15"

WALL OVEN 24" TO 32"

84"

37" TO 45"

24"

WALL OVEN CABINET

SOFFIT 12"

30"

MICROWAVE 18" TYP.

18"

84"

36"

MICROWAVE CABINET

SOFFIT 12"

WALL CAB

MICROWAVE/HOOD COMBINATION UNIT

COOKTOP OR RANGE

USE MFG SPECIFICATIONS

36"

MICROWAVE/HOOD UNIT

4-17
Recommended spacing of wall cabinets above counter-tops and appliances.

wide and 30 inches high." As you plan the height consider what is on the counter below. If it is open counter the wall cabinet is usually placed 18 inches above it. If it is over a range or cooktop, the hood on the bottom is usually 24 inches above the cooking unit. When going over a refrigerator, plan to clear the unit by several inches. A typical refrigerator height is 55 to 65 inches. The bottom of the wall cabinet over the refrigerator is usually placed 69 inches above the floor. Typical design sizes for standard cabinets are in 4-17. Notice the total height of the base plus wall cabinets is typically 7 feet and a 12-inch soffit is furred down. However, you can leave it open above the wall cabinet and use it for decorative objects (4-18). This will require occasional cleaning. You can also run the wall cabinets to the ceiling, providing additional protected storage. However, a small step ladder is needed to reach things.

Typical maximum heights the average person can reach above a 24-inch wide base cabinet and and 12-inch wide shelving, such as in a tall cabinet, are shown in 4-19 and **Table 4-2**.

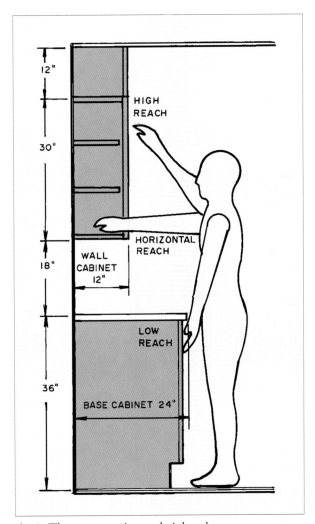

4-19 These are maximum heights the average person can reach above standard cabinets.

4-18 If you leave the space above the wall cabinet open it can serve as a place to display decorative items.

TABLE 4-2 MAXIMUM REACHES FOR PEOPLE OF AVERAGE HEIGHT

REACHES OVER A CABINET (inches)				
Person's height	60	65	72	75
Horizontal forward reach	22	24	25	27
High forward reach	65	70	75	80
Low reach above the floor	26	28	31	33

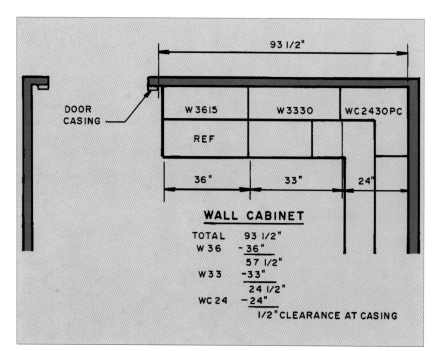

4-20 The wall cabinets on the wall with the door to the garage go over a refrigerator. Leave plenty of room for ventilation and the possibility of sometime installing a larger refrigerator.

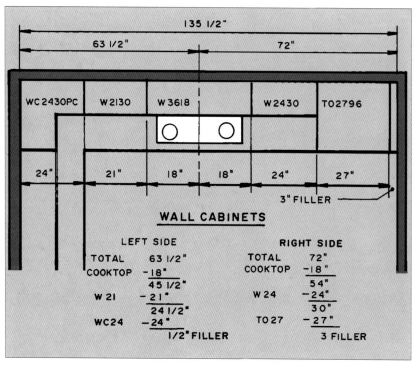

4-21 The wall cabinets on the other side wall support a hood over the cooktop and use a tall oven cabinet in the corner for the wall oven.

Wall cabinet layouts for the other two walls in the example kitchen are in 4-20 and 4-21. In 4-20 you would have to be certain to clear the casing around the door. In 4-21 you have a 24-inch deep wall oven cabinet, so the wall cabinet butts against it. The cabinet over the cooktop is 18 inches high, allowing for a 30-inch clearance above it.

DRAWING THE ELEVATIONS

An elevation drawing is the view looking directly at the wall. If you have a little drafting skill you could work out elevations of each wall of cabinets, such as those shown in 4-22 and 4-23. These drawings will help you visualize the proposed kitchen. Using ¼-inch graph paper will help you make the drawings.

Begin by locating the floor, end walls, countertop, top of the wall cabinets, and ceiling, as shown in 4-22. Then, using the information from the layout drawing, locate the sides of the cabinets and appliances. Finally complete the cabinets by drawing doors and drawers or other details of the cabinetry. This will clearly identify which of the cabinets available you want. You can

CONSTRUCTING KITCHENS

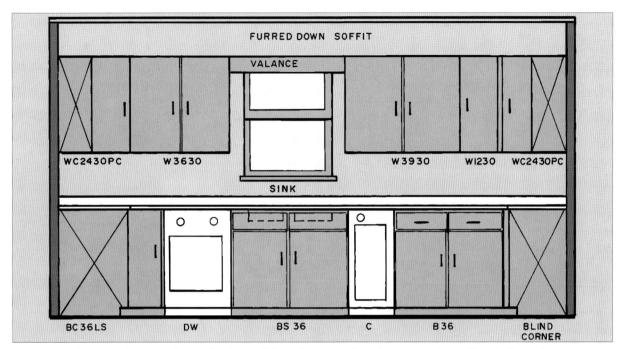

4-22 This elevation drawing shows the faces of the cabinets and appliances on the wall with the sink.

note below each cabinet the manufacturer's identification number for that cabinet or the size information given on the layout drawings. Notes can be added giving information that is not visible, such as sliding shelves or a lazy Susan in a corner cabinet. Be sure to allow for the casings of windows and doors.

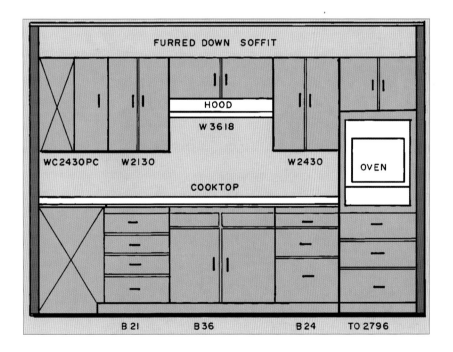

4-23 The elevation drawing shows how the cabinets are placed over the cooktop. The wall oven is set in a tall oven cabinet in the corner.

CHAPTER 5

Kitchen Appliances

The choice of your kitchen appliances is an important factor in your overall satisfaction with the completed kitchen. Visit a number of dealers and keep records of what they say about warranties, costs, and, of great importance, service after the sale. Pick up copies of all the brochures and study them carefully. Visit with friends and see and discuss what they chose and how satisfied they are with the product and the dealer.

Investigate new technical developments to see if they really are as effective as the advertising states. Often they are an improvement over the older traditional appliances. Years ago the microwave oven came on the scene, and now it is difficult to imagine doing without its convenience for certain tasks like reheating and defrosting.

You will have to decide on a color scheme for the kitchen, and in addition to the cabinets the appliances make a major statement. Colors available range from white to black and an extensive range of tans, blues, greens, yellows, and maroons in various hues.

Courtesy Jenn-Aire

5-1 A freestanding range rests on the floor and is slid between the base cabinets. This is a gas-fired range. Notice the controls are on the front so you do not have to reach over the burners to control the level of heat. This is a good size for family use.

The cost of appliances can vary considerably, so consider whether the extra cost provides exceptional quality and performance. Usually it is wise to select high-quality appliances, but this does not always mean high cost.

Complete details on the sizes available are important. You want appliances large enough for the type of cooking and food storage that fits your needs. You also need to fit them in with the cabinets being selected.

The energy used to operate appliances is also a consideration. Cooking units are gas or electric. Gas-fired can use natural gas, if available, or propane. Do you prefer to cook on an electric burner? What types of electric cooking unit are available?

The following pages describe some of the appliances available. You may not choose to use all of them but need to examine each as you reach final decisions.

RANGES

Ranges may be freestanding or drop-in types. The **freestanding range** combines a cooktop, oven, and broiler; some models have a storage drawer at the floor rather than a broiler (5-1). One type has two ovens side by side. A heavy-duty range for those who really enjoy cooking on par with professionals is shown in **5-2**. This has two ovens, gas or electric burners, as well as a barbecue grill. The large top provides space for holding utensils. Freestanding ranges typically are 30 to 36 inches wide though smaller and larger sizes are available. They are insulated to protect the cabinets and retain the heat in the oven. Some types have their own downdraft exhaust systems.

The **drop-in range** is supported by side flanges and fits between base cabinets. It does not rest on the floor (5-3). It has the same features as a freestanding range.

Franke Consumer Products Inc./Kitchen Systems Division

Courtesy Jenn-Aire

5-2 This large freestanding range has two ovens and can have gas or electric burners and a barbecue grill. It is especially valuable for those who enjoy doing a lot of cooking.

5-3 This drop-in range fits snugly between the base cabinets and has a storage area below. This unit has a downdraft ventilator between the cooking units on the top.

COOKTOPS

Courtesy Jenn-Aire

Cooktops are available in gas-fired and electric units (**5-4** and **5-5**). Gas models may have exposed burners, steel or cast-iron grates, or a solid burner cover.

A compact installation of a gas fired cooktop with a gas fired wall oven below is shown in **5-6**. This makes the installation similar to a drop-in range. Electric burners may have an exposed heating element or a solid glass or ceramic top over the elements. Solid disk heating elements are finding increasing use.

Magnetic induction electric cooktops have a heating element that produces a magnetic field causing the steel or cast iron cooking utensil to heat. The cooktop surface is Ceran® glass which remains cool to the touch (**5-7**).

5-4 (Left) This gas-fired cooktop has four burners and a large grill and a downdraft ventilation system.

Courtesy General Electric Appliances

5-5 This electric cooktop recesses neatly into the countertop. The unit is thin enough to allow storage or provide open access below.

Halogen cooktop burners are electric units that produce heat by passing electricity through a filament in a quartz tube. This is infrared light in wavelengths that pass through a glass top. The cooking utensil do not require perfect contact with the glass top, since the cooking action is caused by wavelengths of light that pass through, rather than conduct.

More information on downdraft cooking units is in Chapter 1.

5-6 This gas-fired cooktop also has a gas fired wall oven below, making for a compact installation.

5-7 This cooktop uses magnetic induction to provide radiant heat. It has a ceramic glass surface that enables it to be easily wiped clean.

Indoor barbecue grills are available to fit with the standard base cabinet. They are gas fired and require an adequate hood as recommended by the manufacturer (5-8). Outdoor units for your deck and patio are also popular (5-9). Some ranges and cooktops include the normal burners for everyday cooking plus a grill on the same unit.

WALL OVENS

Wall ovens come in many styles and sizes, as seen in 5-10, 5-11, and 5-12.

5-8 This indoor grill has a downdraft ventilation system. Some also add a hood over the unit.

5-9 This dual-burner outdoor gas grill has stainless-steel rod grates and exterior that keep it looking new over the years and are easily cleaned. It has a rotisserie and storage for tools, seasonings, and utensils.

CONSTRUCTING KITCHENS

5-10 A wall oven is mounted in the cabinet at a height that makes it convenient to use.

Courtesy General Electric Appliances

Courtesy Jenn-Aire

5-11 A typical microwave and wall oven installation. The microwave is placed on top of the wall oven.

Courtesy Jenn-Aire

5-12 A double wall oven is very helpful when you do considerable cooking.

Courtesy Sharp Electronics Corporation

5-13 A typical microwave oven. It heats foods and liquids rapidly and is an almost mandatory appliance.

5-14 (Right) While the microwave is often placed above the range or cooktop, there are many other possible locations for it in the kitchen.

Courtesy Sharp Electronics Corporation

Courtesy Jenn-Aire

5-15 The kitchen has a double wall oven, a separate microwave, and a dishwasher along two walls, forming an efficient layout.

CONSTRUCTING KITCHENS

MICROWAVE OVENS

A microwave oven does not heat the oven space but the microwaves penetrate the food and cause the molecules to oscillate, which generates heat within the food. This heat cooks the food very rapidly but will not form a hard or brown surface as occurs in a conventional oven. A **microwave** is an electromagnetic wave of extremely high frequency. Even though you have a conventional oven, you will want a microwave oven because it will speed up preparation of many foods that only require heating, such as frozen TV dinners or quantities of liquid (5-13). If you want to bake cookies, you need your conventional oven. Microwaves are frequently installed above the range or cooktop (5-14) but can be placed anywhere. Consider putting a small one in a recreation room.

In **5-15** notice the relationship between the microwave and double oven. The microwave is placed in an angled corner cabinet, making it centrally located.

REFRIGERATOR/ FREEZERS

The typical refrigerator is a freestanding appliance usually consisting of a freezer compartment and a refrigeration compartment that keeps food cool but does not freeze it. Possibly the most frequently chosen style has the freezer and refrigeration compartments side by side (5-16), but some appliances have the freezer on the top (5-17) or bottom. You can buy separate freezers to store larger quantities of food. Some refrigerators have ice makers and supply chilled beverages with a faucet outside the unit.

Courtesy Whirlpool Corporation

5-16 A typical refrigerator/freezer with side-by-side freezer and refrigeration compartments.

5-17 A refrigerator/freezer with the freezing compartment across the top of the unit. Notice the microwave above the freestanding range.

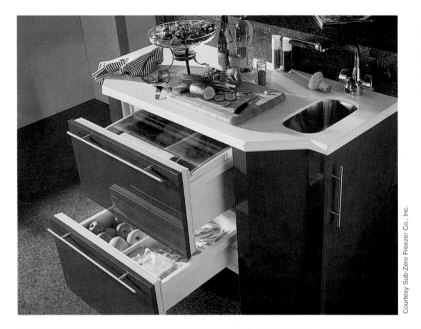

5-18 Small refrigerator drawers fit below a standard counter. These units are used in the contemporary kitchen as well as in recreation rooms and entertainment areas.

Courtesy Sub-Zero Freezer Co., Inc.

Courtesy Sub-Zero Freezer Co., Inc.

5-19 The cabinetwork of this side-by-side refrigerator/freezer makes it an attractive part of the kitchen.

Courtesy Sub-Zero Freezer Co., Inc.

5-20 This refrigerator/freezer has paneled doors that blend in perfectly with the wall paneling.

CONSTRUCTING KITCHENS

Small under-the-counter refrigerators are available to use to provide a second source of frozen or cooled foods in the kitchen or in a recreation room for refreshments when entertaining. They make ice cubes and provide a cooled compartment (5-18).

Deluxe refrigerator/freezers have the doors built to match or at least complement the cabinets and tone down the kitchen look. The unit in **5-19** has wood-paneled doors, making it an attractive installation. Another approach is shown in **5-20**. While it clearly is a refrigerator/freezer, the paneling on the doors blends in perfectly with the wall paneling.

DISHWASHERS

Dishwashers are now almost automatically installed in the kitchen, as are the range and refrigerator (5-21). They are very convenient and, most importantly, produce clean, germ-free dishes—much better than the old hand wash and dry, using a dish towel whose cleanliness is always in question. They are sized to fit in the

5-21 This dishwasher is installed to the right of the sink. Notice how the cabinets and resilient floor covering blend, giving prominence to the dishwasher and sink.

Courtesy Congoleum Corporation

standard base cabinet and require a hot water connection, a waste line, and electricity. They have short and normal wash cycles, a plate warmer cycle and a rinse only and hold cycle. They have heated drying. They require 15- to 20-amp circuit breakers and 120V service. The inlet hot water should be at least 120°F.

The racks of the dishwasher are plastic coated to protect the dishes, and they slide out for easy loading and unloading (**5-22**).

Courtesy Jenn-Aire

5-22 The dishwasher is marked by convenience, including plastic-coated sliding racks to protect the dishes and make loading and unloading easy.

CONSTRUCTING KITCHENS

COMPACTORS

Trash compactors compress trash into a relatively solid mass, thus reducing the volume of the material to be disposed about 75%. They require 12 to 18 inches of space in the base cabinet beside the sink. Some prefer to locate it a few feet away from the sink. They require 120V electric service.

GARBAGE DISPOSALS

Garbage disposals are installed below a sink, as seen in (5-23). Usually it is in a second bowl of a two- or three-bowl sink. The main sink is largest so it goes below the smaller sink. They require 120V electric service and a waste line connected to the same line used by the sinks. The water from the dishwasher is run through the disposal and discharges through the same waste pipe. In some areas they are not permitted by codes, so check your local building codes.

5-23 Garbage disposals are mounted below one of the sinks.

CHAPTER 6

Electrical Requirements

Courtesy Lithonia Lighting

The kitchen has need for considerable electrical power. The actual circuits and loads are figured by the electrician after you show on the plan where you want lights, outlets, and service to the appliances (**6-1**). The power ratings on the appliances must be known so the proper-size wiring can be used and the required voltage supplied.

Some appliances, all lights, and wall outlets require 120V current. Other appliances, such as a range, require 240V.

If you are remodeling an older house, the power delivered to the service entrance panel may be as small as 60A (amperes). You will have to have an electrician upgrade this service to 100A or more as required by the new appliances. A new house will typically have a 150A to 200A service entrance. Check your local building codes for specific requirements.

6-1 The locations of the lights and appliances will be detailed on the plan of the kitchen, including the locations of the refrigerator and recessed and surface-mounted lights such as those featured in this kitchen.

TABLE 6-1 TYPICAL REQUIREMENTS FOR ELECTRICAL CIRCUITS

Small Appliance Circuits	Voltage	120V	Special-Purpose Circuits	Voltage	240V
	Amperage	20A		Amperage	30A
	Wire size	No. 12 copper		Wire size	No. 10 copper
	Use	Serves small appliances, such as toasters, radio, TV, mixer. This circuit will have fewer outlets than general-purpose circuits because appliances take more current.		Use	Large appliances, such as ranges and ovens
			General-Purpose Circuits	Voltage	120V
				Amperage	20A
				Wire size	No. 12 copper
				Use	Lights and wall receptacles

AMPERES, VOLTS & WATTS

An **ampere** is a unit of the **rate of flow** of electric current. This is in general similar to the number of gallons of water that will flow through a pipe. The electric current is under **pressure**, similar to water in a pipe being under pressure. The unit of **electrical pressure** is the **volt**. The **amount of power** in a circuit is given in **watts**. A watt is the result of volts × amperes (flow × pressure).

LOCATING ELECTRIC RECEPTACLES

Generally you will have small appliances, general-purpose, and special-purpose circuits. Typical requirements are given in **Table 6-1**.

The National Electrical Code specifies that the walls of the kitchen without cabinets should have receptacles located so that no point along the floor line is horizontally more than 6 feet from an outlet. The 6-foot measurement starts at a door or other break in the wall. The measurement is permitted to go around corners, thus including parts of two walls. These outlets are on 120V/20A circuits and will operate lamps, radios, televisions, and other 120V appliances. Any isolated section of wall at least 2 feet or more in width should have a receptacle.

Receptacles installed above the countertop should be spaced every 4 feet or closer. They should not be located more than 18 inches above the top and must be recessed in the wall. They should never be placed faceup in a countertop. Any countertop 12 inches or wider should have a receptacle. The receptacles over countertops should be supplied by at least two small appliance circuits. You should always check your local electric code.

There are other requirements specified in the National Electrical Code that must be observed by the electrician as circuits are designed. The number of receptacles allowed by code permits more to be on a general-purpose circuit than on an appliance circuit.

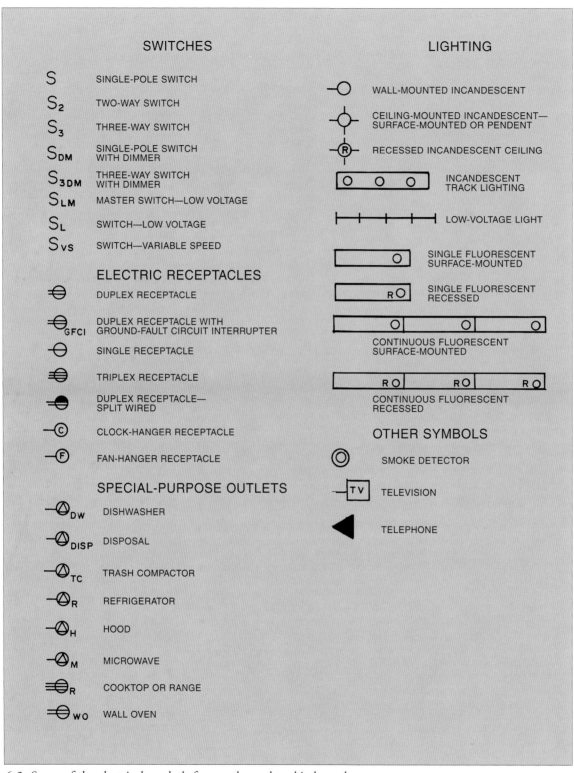

SWITCHES

S — SINGLE-POLE SWITCH

S_2 — TWO-WAY SWITCH

S_3 — THREE-WAY SWITCH

S_{DM} — SINGLE-POLE SWITCH WITH DIMMER

S_{3DM} — THREE-WAY SWITCH WITH DIMMER

S_{LM} — MASTER SWITCH—LOW VOLTAGE

S_L — SWITCH—LOW VOLTAGE

S_{VS} — SWITCH—VARIABLE SPEED

ELECTRIC RECEPTACLES

DUPLEX RECEPTACLE

DUPLEX RECEPTACLE WITH GROUND-FAULT CIRCUIT INTERRUPTER

SINGLE RECEPTACLE

TRIPLEX RECEPTACLE

DUPLEX RECEPTACLE— SPLIT WIRED

CLOCK-HANGER RECEPTACLE

FAN-HANGER RECEPTACLE

SPECIAL-PURPOSE OUTLETS

DISHWASHER

DISPOSAL

TRASH COMPACTOR

REFRIGERATOR

HOOD

MICROWAVE

COOKTOP OR RANGE

WALL OVEN

LIGHTING

WALL-MOUNTED INCANDESCENT

CEILING-MOUNTED INCANDESCENT— SURFACE-MOUNTED OR PENDENT

RECESSED INCANDESCENT CEILING

INCANDESCENT TRACK LIGHTING

LOW-VOLTAGE LIGHT

SINGLE FLUORESCENT SURFACE-MOUNTED

SINGLE FLUORESCENT RECESSED

CONTINUOUS FLUORESCENT SURFACE-MOUNTED

CONTINUOUS FLUORESCENT RECESSED

OTHER SYMBOLS

SMOKE DETECTOR

TELEVISION

TELEPHONE

6-2 Some of the electrical symbols frequently used on kitchen plans.

Receptacles and other electrical fixtures are indicated on your plan drawing with the symbols shown in **6-2**.

GROUND-FAULT CIRCUIT INTERRUPTERS

A ground-fault circuit interrupter (GFCI) is a device that monitors the amount of current going to a load (such as a dishwasher) and compares it with the amount leaving the appliance. If the two amounts are equal, the electricity is flowing properly. However, if some of the electrons are missing on the flow away from the appliance, the current leaving is less than that going into it. Therefore there is a leakage in the system. The GFCI detects this difference and opens the circuit. This leakage is too small to trip a circuit breaker or blow a fuse, yet current is leaking from the circuit. This could be running through the person using the appliance to a ground. It is actually a short in the circuit. The GFCI will open the circuit in $\frac{1}{30}$ of a second, keeping you from getting a bad shock. The imbalance of current flow that the GFCI detects is four to six milliamps (thousandths of an ampere). This means you might get a shock but it will only last for $\frac{1}{30}$ of a second. Most people can withstand this shock before their heart goes into fibrillation. Fibrillation is when the heart goes out of sync, resulting in death.

Building codes specify where GFCI protection must be installed, and the kitchen with many electrical appliances and water is one place it should be used. Codes require all countertop receptacles within a 6-foot straight-line distance from a sink to have GFCI protection Check your local code to verify the requirements.

GFCI TYPES

For your residence you can have a circuit-breaker GFCI or use receptacle GFCI. The **circuit-breaker GFCI** is mounted in the service entrance panel and provides protection on all receptacles on that circuit. The **receptacle GFCI** is placed in the outlet box instead of a standard convenience outlet. It protects only those things plugged into that one receptacle. It looks like a standard receptacle but has a test and reset button. If the appliance plugged into it trips it, you can unplug the appliance and restore power to the receptacle by pressing the reset button (**6-3**). The receptacle can be tested by pressing the test button and reset by pressing the reset button.

KITCHEN LIGHTING

As you plan the kitchen lighting, remember you will need **general lighting** to provide an overall illumination of the room. You will also need **task lighting** to put additional light in a specific area, such as a sink, that is not adequately lighted by the general lighting sources. You can also use **special lighting** to enhance a feature or provide dramatic illumination of some aspect of the kitchen, such as illuminating a cathedral ceiling.

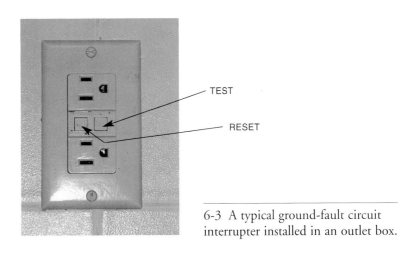

6-3 A typical ground-fault circuit interrupter installed in an outlet box.

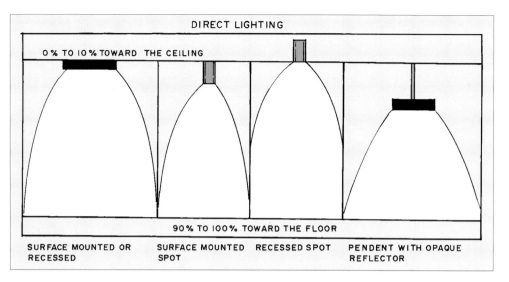

DIRECT LIGHTING

0% TO 10% TOWARD THE CEILING

90% TO 100% TOWARD THE FLOOR

SURFACE MOUNTED OR RECESSED | SURFACE MOUNTED SPOT | RECESSED SPOT | PENDENT WITH OPAQUE REFLECTOR

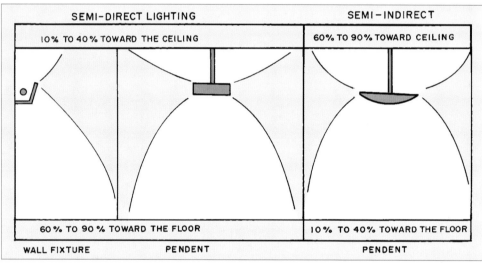

SEMI-DIRECT LIGHTING

10% TO 40% TOWARD THE CEILING

60% TO 90% TOWARD THE FLOOR

WALL FIXTURE | PENDENT

SEMI-INDIRECT

60% TO 90% TOWARD CEILING

10% TO 40% TOWARD THE FLOOR

PENDENT

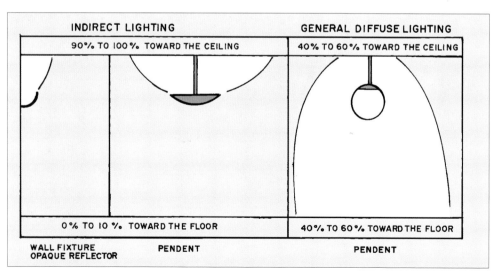

INDIRECT LIGHTING

90% TO 100% TOWARD THE CEILING

0% TO 10% TOWARD THE FLOOR

WALL FIXTURE OPAQUE REFLECTOR | PENDENT

GENERAL DIFFUSE LIGHTING

40% TO 60% TOWARD THE CEILING

40% TO 60% TOWARD THE FLOOR

PENDENT

6-4 The type of fixture and its location influences how the light is distributed.

The type of fixture and its placement will control how much light is directed to the ceiling and how much is directed down to the floor (**6-4**).

Direct lighting provides the most illumination toward the floor and produces more glare than the other types. **Semidirect** illuminaries put some light on the ceiling but most toward the floor. The **indirect** and **semi-indirect illuminaries** have an opaque reflector that directs most light to the ceiling, relying on reflected light to illuminate the room and produce the least glare. **General diffuse illuminaries** balance the light about equally between the floor and ceiling.

As you make decisions consider that it is better to use several lower-wattage lights spaced apart than one high-wattage fixture in the center of the room (**6-5**). Also remember that fluorescent lights produce about 2½ times the light output of incandescent bulbs. For example, two 100-watt incandescent bulbs can be replaced with two F40 fluorescent tubes. In general you can figure the total wattage needed by multiplying the square feet in the room by 2 or 3 watts per square foot. As you select light fixtures, note the maximum-wattage bulb they will take. For example, a 100-watt bulb should never be used in a fixture with a maximum rating of 60 watts. This is a fire hazard. Diffused and indirect lighting tend to be more evenly distributed and produce less glare than direct light. Direct light tends to reduce the shadows produced by diffused and indirect light, so a combination of these carefully placed will produce the best results.

GENERAL LIGHTING

General lighting is usually provided by surface-mounted or recessed fluorescent fixtures or a luminous ceiling. The fluorescent fixtures may be a dropped type or closed case that fits flat against the ceiling (**6-6**). The dropped fixture has

Courtesy Lithonia Lighting

6-5 In large kitchens it is usually best to install several lower-wattage lights than one large fixture with higher-wattage lamps.

Courtesy Lithonia Lighting

6-6 Surface-mounted fluorescent fixtures are frequently used to provide general illumination.

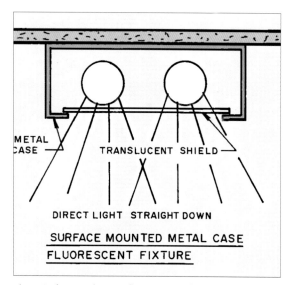
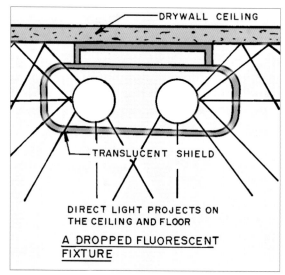

META CASE

TRANSLUCENT SHIELD

DIRECT LIGHT STRAIGHT DOWN

SURFACE MOUNTED METAL CASE FLUORESCENT FIXTURE

DRYWALL CEILING

TRANSLUCENT SHIELD

DIRECT LIGHT PROJECTS ON THE CEILING AND FLOOR

A DROPPED FLUORESCENT FIXTURE

6-7 A dropped-type fluorescent fixture mounted on the ceiling will provide some indirect lighting as well as direct lighting, creating a more pleasant illumination that direct alone.

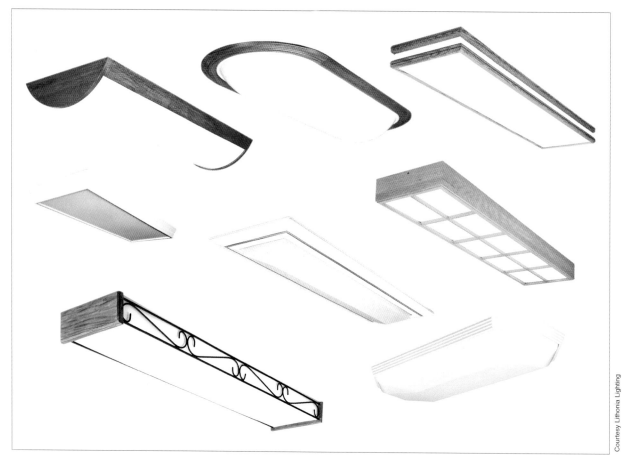

6-8 Some of the ypes of surface-mounted fluorescent fixture available.

Courtesy Lithonia Lighting

CONSTRUCTING KITCHENS

the advantage of giving some indirect light off the ceiling. The closed-case fixture provides direct light down only and produces more glare. In general recessed lights do not produce the quality of light you want for general illumination (**6-7**). Surface-mounted fluorescent fixtures are available in many styles, so select one that fits in with the overall decor of your kitchen (**6-8**).

General lighting can also be provided by recessed downlights. Be certain you select fixtures that meet the codes and also meet fire regulations. When covered with insulation, lower-wattage bulbs must be used. Some build a box around the fixture to keep the insulation 3 inches away. Two types of recessed fixture are shown in **6-9**.

The recessed fixtures can be spaced conveniently across the ceiling to provide the desired footcandles of light toward the floor (**6-10**). Recessed fixtures also can be used for task and decorative lighting.

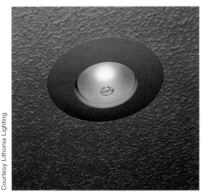

6-9 Two types of recessed downlight fixture.

6-10 Recessed downlighting provides general illumination in this kitchen.

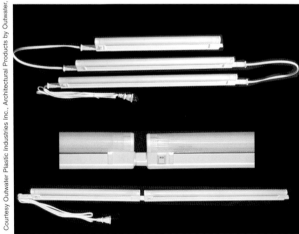

6-11 Special lights are available for mounting below the wall cabinet, providing task lighting for the countertop. Notice also the use of recessed fixtures for general lighting in the top view of kitchen wall cabinets that have special task lights mounted beneath them.

TASK LIGHTING

Task lighting is used to provide increased illumination in areas where work is to be performed. Special fluorescent fixtures are made that are mounted under the cabinet (**6-11**). They are often located near the front of the cabinet (**6-12**). The fixture should be covered by the faceframe of the cabinet or a strip added to conceal it. On frameless cabinets it is often installed near the center or rear of the cabinet to conceal it. This limits how far the light projects to the edge of the counter but in most cases is adequate.

You can also locate recessed incandescent lights in the cabinet or soffit above a sink as shown in **6-13**. If they are surface mounted they can be

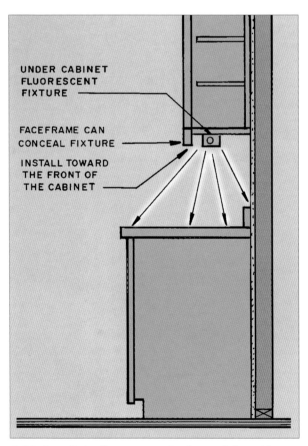

UNDER CABINET
FLUORESCENT
FIXTURE

FACEFRAME CAN
CONCEAL FIXTURE

INSTALL TOWARD
THE FRONT OF
THE CABINET

6-12 Install the fixture near the front of the cabinet.

hidden with the valance. This improves the appearance and blocks the glare from your face as you work at the sink. In all cases fluorescent tubes should be covered with a plastic shield to protect them from possible breakage. The fixtures should be rated safe for direct contact with the wood cabinets or other combustible materials.

The kitchen dining area usually needs additional lighting. A pendant fixture on a chain or pipe pendant over the table is a good way to handle this situation (6-14). Keep the light about 36 inches above the table. The higher the light is above the table, the wider the circle of light around the table. If it is too high it could bother those at the table. In all cases the fixture should not have exposed bulbs. Some form of translucent globe or cover over the bulbs is necessary. The use of a dimmer switch is a big asset. Generally 100 to 120 watts is enough for this situation.

Courtesy Thomas Lighting

6-13 These incandescent spots are recessed into the soffit above the sink.

6-14 Pendant lights are an easy way to light the kitchen dining area. They do not require a high-wattage bulb. The bulb should be covered with a translucent shield.

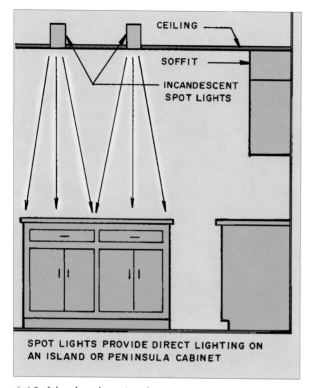

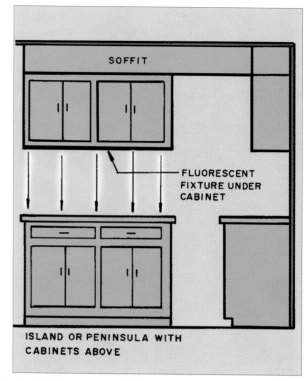

SPOT LIGHTS PROVIDE DIRECT LIGHTING ON AN ISLAND OR PENINSULA CABINET

ISLAND OR PENINSULA WITH CABINETS ABOVE

6-15 Island and peninsula counters require some type of task lighting. Recessed downlights work well for islands and peninsulas without cabinets above; fluorescent strips can be used when there are cabinets above.

Courtesy Thomas Lighting

If you have an island counter or a peninsula you will need to provide some form of task lighting from above. You might use recessed or track lighting above the island or peninsula, if it does not have directly cabinets above (6-15). Another approach when there are no cabinets above is to use a pendant light or lights to provide additional general light as well as to increase the task light available as shown in 6-16.

6-16 Pendant lights can be used to increase the illumination of island and peninsula counters.

SPECIALTY LIGHTING

While specialty lighting can contribute to general illumination and task lighting, the main purpose is to provide a focus on selected details of the room. For example, valance, sconce (**6-17**), and cove lights provide light on the ceiling around the room. These are usually very low-wattage to produce a warm glow (**6-18**).

Track lighting is another way to provide attention to some feature of a kitchen. The track is secured to the wall or ceiling and the lampholders are installed where you want them along the track. The lampholders can be rotated to the position and angle desired. These are very flexible fixtures and provide dramatic accents to kitchen features (**6-19**). Dimmer switches on specialty lighting will let you vary the brightness, thus increasing the possible visual enhancements.

Courtesy Outwater Plastic Industries Inc., Architectural Products by Outwater, LLC

6-17 A sconce is one type of accent light that provides a subtle glow to the kitchen.

6-18 These lights can provide accent lighting, enhancing the overall appearance of the kitchen. They need not be high-wattage units.

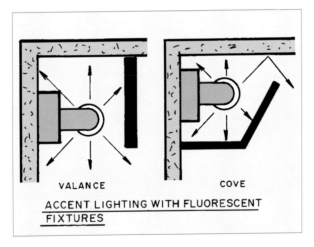

VALANCE   COVE

ACCENT LIGHTING WITH FLUORESCENT FIXTURES

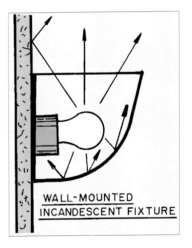

WALL-MOUNTED INCANDESCENT FIXTURE

6-19 Track lighting can be used for general illumination, as well as for decorative lighting.

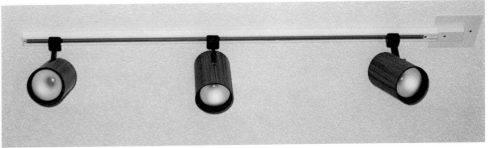

Another accent lighting fixture is a recessed unit often referred to as an "eyeball" because the flood or spotlight bulb is in a round metal case that can be revolved, directing the light in many directions. It is often used in soffits and ceilings (**6-20**).

Another decorative type of lighting is a product called rope lighting. This unique form of lighting is a flexible vinyl rope with spaced individual lights that is easy to install, attractive, and simple to move when necessary. In **6-21** it has been used along the top of a set of wall cabinets.

TYPES OF LAMP

The types of lamp available that are used in kitchens include fluorescent, incandescent, low-voltage, and tungsten-halogen.

Fluorescent lamps have a long glass tube filled with an inert gas, such as argon, and low-pressure mercury vapor. A cathode is on each end. The cathode produces electrons that start and maintain operation of a mercury arc which produces an ultraviolet arc. The ultraviolet arc is absorbed by phosphors coating the inside of the tube and causes it to fluoresce (radiate) light.

6-20 This recessed fixture allows you to rotate the light in many directions. Another example is seen in 6-9.

Courtesy Outwater Plastic Industries Inc., Architectural Products by Outwater, LLC

6-21 Rope lighting provides an attractive decorative touch to cabinets and other architectural features.

They are available in straight tubes, circles, and U-shapes (**6-22**). A flourescent lamp that screws into a standard socket is also available.

Incandescent lamps have a filament inside a glass bulb joined to a metal base. The tungsten wire filament resists the flow of electricity and thus gets hot and glows, producing light. Such lamps are rated in watts and made with several different base diameters (**6-23**).

Tungsten-halogen lamps have a tungsten filament and are filled with a halogen gas, such as iodine or bromine, in combination with an inert gas. The bulb is made from quartz because quartz is able to withstand the higher temperatures produced by this lamp (**6-24**). The tungsten-halogen lamp has a screw-type base. Since this type of lamp operates at high temperatures, it requires a protective envelope.

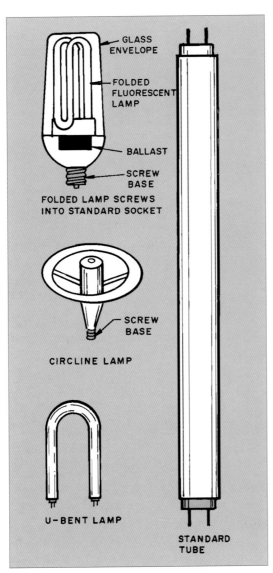

6-22 Fluorescent lamps are available in several shapes. Some screw into a standard lamp socket.

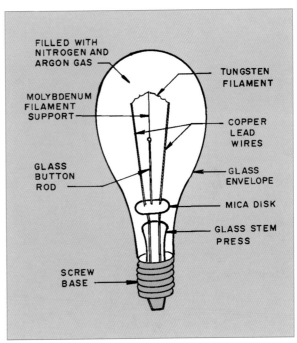

6-23 The construction of a typical incandescent lamp.

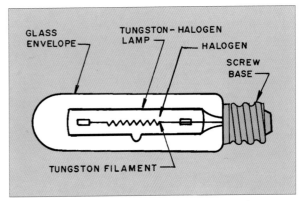

6-24 A typical screw-type tungsten-halogen lamp.

Courtesy Outwater Plastic Industries Inc., Architectural Products by Outwater, LLC

6-25 This low-voltage lighting system operates on a 12-volt transformer. It is easily moved whenever a change is desired.

Low-voltage systems have a transformer that lowers the standard 120V to generally 24V. The low-voltage bulbs produce less heat and give a light with good color rendition. The ambiance lighting in **6-25** operates on 12 volts and is run by a transformer. It can be used to highlight a feature or create a pool of light in a dark area.

CHOOSING LAMPS

As you consider various lamps, consider the wattage and the lumens. **Wattage** is the measure of electrical consumption of the lamp and **lumens** describes the amount of light produced measured at the lamp. Another measure is **foot-candles**, which is the amount of light received at the surface being lighted. It is equal to 1 lumen per square foot. For example, a standard incandescent lamp delivers 5 to 20 lumens per watt, while a fluorescent lamp delivers 60 to 100 lumens.

Lamps also have a range of color characteristics. The color of light is measured in degrees Kelvin (metric unit for temperature) and the Color Rendition Index (CRI). Typical incandescent lamps have a color temperature of around 2700°K. They have a tone of reds, oranges, and yellows. This is described as a warm tone.

Fluorescent lamps available range from about 3000° to 7500°K. Those at the higher temperatures tend toward blue and green tones and are referred to as cool colors.

Halogen lamps average about 3000°K and are whiter than incandescent but warmer than most fluorescent.

In your kitchen, try to select lamps that are close to each other in color temperature. Do not mix warm incandescents with the upper-temperature fluorescents. Instead select a lower-temperature fluorescent lamp.

The **Color Rendition Index** (**CRI**) is based on a scale of 100. It indicates how nearly true the color of an object appears under a particular lamp. For most natural colors choose a lamp that has a CRI near 100. A rating near 100 indicates the light is near daylight. The CRI of various lamps is indicated in the lamp charts provided by the manufacturer.

124   CONSTRUCTING KITCHENS

LIGHTING CONTROLS

The most commonly used switch is a single-pole, single-throw switch. It operates one light or a series of connected lights from one location. Often it is desirable to be able to operate some of the lights, especially those used for general illumination, from two different locations. To do this use a three-way switch. It will turn the light on and off from two locations. A light can be controlled from three locations by using two three-way switches and one four-way switch (**6-26**).

Special-effects lighting can be enhanced by using a dimmer switch. The intensity of the light produced can be varied from off to full brightness by turning the dimmer switch knob (**6-27**). Different switches are required for incandescent and fluorescent fixtures.

6-27 Dimmer switches are used to increase and decrease the amount of light produced. This one is rotated to vary the intensity of the light. Some types have a lever that is moved up and down.

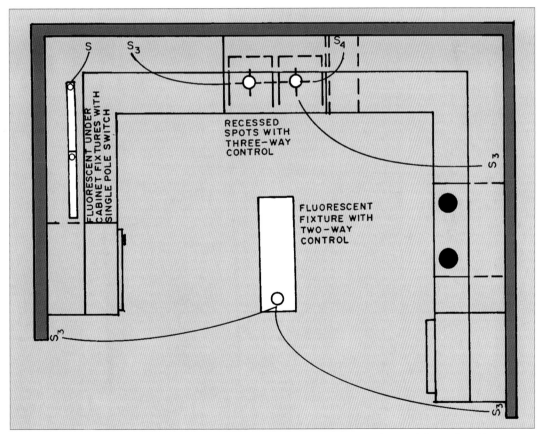

6-26 Lights can be controlled from two locations with two-way switches and from three locations with three-way switches.

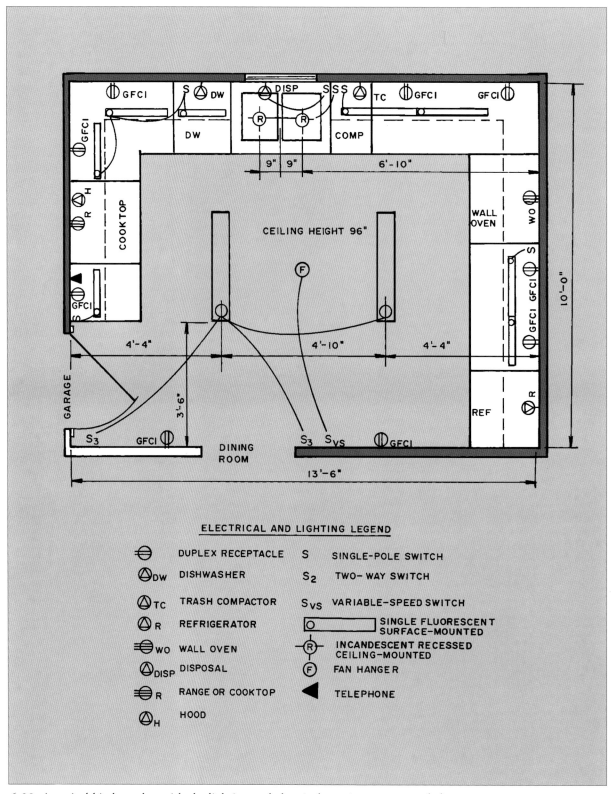

6-28 A typical kitchen plan with the lighting and electrical requirements recorded.

CONSTRUCTING KITCHENS

DRAWING
THE ELECTRICAL &
LIGHTING PLAN

Typically the floor plan used for the electrical and lighting plan is a copy of the detailed plan that shows the locations of cabinets and appliances. Some architects or designers prefer to show dimensions giving room size and locating appliances and cabinets. Others will locate the symbols right on the cabinet drawing. You may want to show plumbing, heating, air conditioning, and ventilation systems on the same plan. A typical electrical and lighting plan is shown in **6-28**. A legend identifying the symbols used is included. Typical symbols in use are shown earlier in **6-2**. The specifications detailing the brand, specific type, and other details identifying each light fixture are listed separately on a light fixture schedule.

This plan locates the lights by dimensions from the walls of the room and between fixtures. It shows all the required receptacles and other electrical connections. The lights are connected to switches with a curved line, and a curved line also connects all lights controlled by one switch.

CEILING
FANS

In many parts of the country a large-diameter ceiling fan is a standard part of the electrical plan (**6-29**). These fans are used in all rooms and are very useful in the kitchen to move the air in a uniform flow. They also help the heating and air-conditioning to be more effective. Notice the fan symbol on the electric plan in **6-28**. The use of a variable-speed wall switch makes it easy to adjust the speed. Most fans have four or five speeds.

6-29 Ceiling fans are used to move the air in a kitchen. They assist with both heating and air-conditioning. In the summer they can be set to rotate so that they blow down, and in the winter, so they blow up to the ceiling.

CHAPTER 7

Plumbing Fixtures & Connections

The kitchen sink is the center of the food preparation and clean-up activities. It is used as a source of drinking water, a place to wash vegetables and dishes, and a place to wash your hands. Possibly it is the most used of the appliances and fixtures in the kitchen. In large kitchens a small secondary sink is often placed in a location away from the main sink, such as at an island or peninsula counter. This makes the kitchen layout more efficient.

There are many types of kitchen sink available, and sizes, features, and materials vary. Since a sink is so important to efficient kitchen operation, time should be spent examining the choices available so you get the one that best serves your needs.

SINKS

Kitchen sinks are available in various sizes of single, double, and triple bowls and have two, three, or four openings for sprays (7-1), faucets (7-2), and soap/lotion dispensers (7-3). The manufacturer specifies the minimum length of cabinet needed for the installation of each of their sinks. This typically ranges from 24 to 48 inches. Some have drainboards on one side. Sinks are available with the main bowl on the left or right side, so you will have to decide which serves you the best.

Courtesy Franke Consumer Products, Inc., Kitchen Systems Division

7-1 Sprays are a very useful accessory at the kitchen sink for food preparation as well as cleanup.

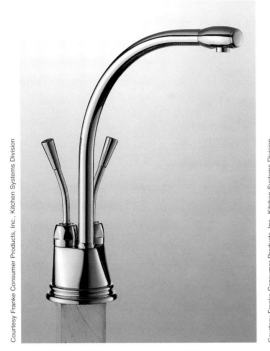

Courtesy Franke Consumer Products, Inc., Kitchen Systems Division

7-2 One of the many types of kitchen sink faucet available. Others are shown in the photographs in this chapter.

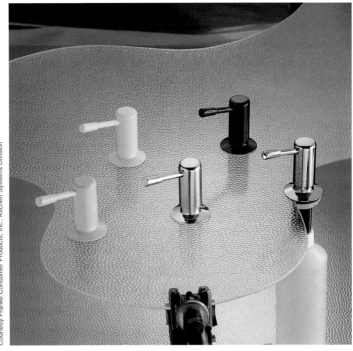

Courtesy Franke Consumer Products, Inc., Kitchen Systems Division

7-3 These dispensers are mounted on kitchen sinks. They are used for soap and hand lotion.

SINGLE BOWL SINKS

Single bowl sinks are often used as a second sink in a large kitchen or as the main sink in a small kitchen with limited cabinet countertop area. It has one drain. A disposal can be mounted on this drain. When you choose a single-bowl sink, try to get one large enough to hold the larger utensils you plan to use (7-4). A single sink 22 inches deep and 25 inches long is a good choice for the main sink when space is limited. A nice size secondary single sink is 22 inches deep and 17 inches long. However, smaller sizes are available. A single-bowl sink will usually require a 30-inch cabinet.

Courtesy The Swan Corporation

7-4 This single-bowl sink is made from a reinforced, modified acrylic filled with natural materials. You drill holes in for faucets, sprays, and soap/lotion dispensers.

7-5 This two-bowl sink has bowls of the same size and matching faucets, spray, and soap/lotion dispenser.

7-6 This stainless-steel two-bowl sink has one smaller bowl. The disposal is usually connected to this bowl.

CONSTRUCTING KITCHENS

7-7 This stainless-steel sink has a drainboard on one side. One bowl is large enough to hold a dish-drying rack.

TWO-BOWL SINKS

Two-bowl sinks are probably the most widely used and a good choice for the main sink. A disposal is mounted on one bowl. Some have bowls of equal size (7-5) and others a smaller bowl for the disposal (7-6). A good size is 22 inches × 33 inches. However, other sizes are available. Some styles have an integral drainboard on one side (7-7). The drainboard can be on the left or right side. A two-bowl sink will usually require a 36- to 48-inch cabinet.

CORNER SINKS

A corner sink is a two-bowl fixture used where the countertop turns a corner (7-8). Often corner windows are installed, providing

7-8 A corner sink fits diagonally in the corner formed by the intersection of the base cabinets.

Courtesy ACT, Inc., D'Mand® Systems

7-9 Corner sinks are enhanced if corner windows are used.

Courtesy Avonite, Inc.

7-10 This sink is made of a nonporous, homogeneous blend of a polyester resin and natural minerals.

natural light and an attractive installation (7-9). They typically require a 36-inch cabinet.

THREE-BOWL SINKS

If you have a large kitchen and do a lot of food preparation, a three-bowl sink is a real help. A three-bowl sink will usually require a 48-inch cabinet. Some three-bowl sinks also have a drainboard. They typically have a small sink for a disposal in the center and a large sink on each side.

SINK MATERIALS

Sinks are available made from stainless steel, porcelain enamel on cast iron or steel, and man-made composite materials such as Corian® and Swanstone®.

Stainless-steel sinks come in several thicknesses of metal and you need to look at these and decide which you want. The heavier the gauge, the more durable the fixture. They do not chip like enamel sinks but do show water spots, will scratch with the use of kitchen abrasives and cleaning pads, and some chemicals may cause them to discolor. You can buy cleaners at the local food stores designed for use on stainless steel sinks. A stainless-steel sink is seen earlier in 7-6.

Porcelain enamel sinks are widely used and enable you to select from a variety of colors. Those made from pressed steel cost less than those made of cast iron, but they are not as durable.

Pressed-steel sinks are lighter weight. The enamel will chip if hit by a heavy object, such as a dropped piece of silverware. You can buy repair kits to seal and color chips, but you never get a repair as good as the sink was before it was chipped. If you do not repair a chip, you may get the spot to start rusting.

Enamel sinks clean easily with standard non-abrasive cleaners and do not tend to scratch.

Molded kitchen sinks are becoming widely used and are made from composite materials such as quartz composites, granite composites, or reinforced, modified acrylic or polyester resins. The sink in **7-10** is a composite made from natural minerals and a polyester resin. The color and pattern run completely through the material so that as the surface is worn the same color is still visible. Severly damaged areas can be cut away and replaced or sanded smooth. The area is then buffed blending in the repair. The material resists chipping, fracture, and cracking.

The **quartz composite** is a blend of quartz (a natural mineral) bonded in a plastic resin. The color is clear and it will not chip or peel.

The **granite composite** is made by bonding fired granite (a natural material) in a plastic resin compound. It produces colors in the natural tones of the granite. It resists stains, scratches, and chips and is very durable.

Swanstone® is a homogeneous, nonporous material with color molded throughout. It is a reinforced, modified acrylic filled with natural minerals. It is cleaned with normal kitchen and bath detergents. Scratches can be sanded away with a fine-grit abrasive. It will not chip, peel, or stain (**7-11**).

7-11 This two-bowl sink is a solid composite material made from reinforced, modified acrylic filled with natural minerals. This sink is mounted under the countertop.

Courtesy The Swan Corporation

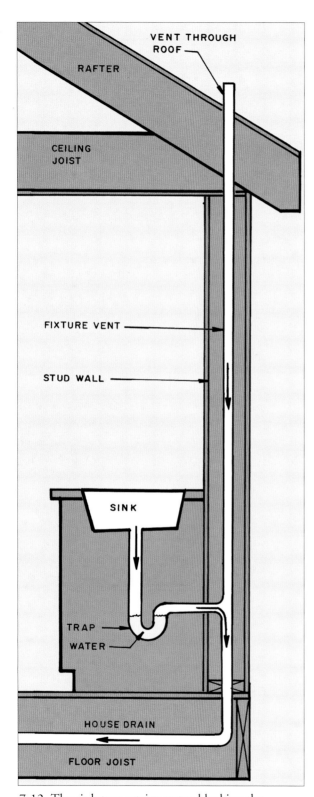

SINK PLUMBING

The sink waste line connects to the building waste system at a stub that comes through the wall below the sink. A **P-trap** is inserted between the sink drain and the wall stub (7-12). The trap fills with water, which keeps sewer gases from running back up the waste pipe into the room through the sink drain. The fixture has a vent pipe, or stack, running from the connection of the sink drain through the roof. This permits the waste disposal system to operate at atmospheric pressure. If a vent is not provided, the water in the trap can be siphoned out when another fixture is used, thus letting sewer gas into the room. A typical installation using plastic pipe is shown in 7-13. Plastic waste pipe is almost universally used.

Other appliances such as the dishwasher and disposal are connected into the waste line below the sink along with the sink waste line. Follow the manufacturer's instructions (7-14).

7-13 A typical P-trap as used on kitchen sinks.

7-12 The sink trap retains water, blocking the entrance of sewer gas into the kitchen.

RAPID HOT WATER SERVICE

Often a sink or appliance is a long way from the hot water heater. At the sink it is annoying to have to run the hot water line awhile before you get hot water. This also wastes water and some of the energy used to heat the hot water that remains unused in the pipe to the sink.

There are a number of products available to help. One system uses a small water tank that is kept full by a connection to the cold water line. The tank is installed below the sink and the water in it is kept hot by its electric coil. This provides a small amount of hot water immediately.

If you want a more generous source, you can install a small water heater near the sink or use one of the systems that uses a pump to move the cooled water in the hot water line back to the

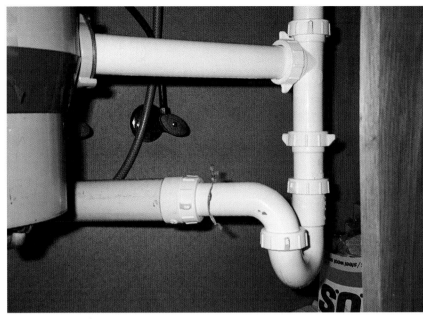

7-14 This disposal is connected to the sink waste line.

water heater. In **7-15** is a rapid hot water supply system that moves hot water from the water heater to the most remote fixture. As you push the activation button, a pump starts and moves

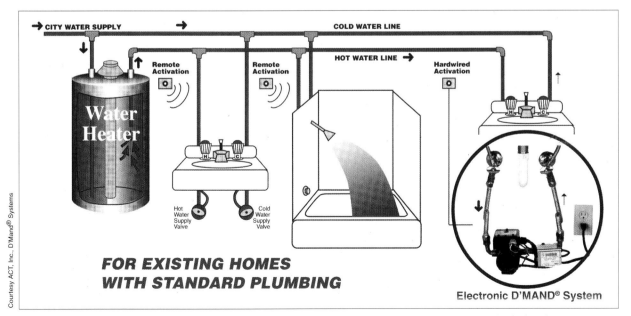

Courtesy ACT, Inc., D'Mand® Systems

FOR EXISTING HOMES WITH STANDARD PLUMBING

Electronic D'MAND® System

7-15 This rapid hot water system is designed to be installed for existing homes with standard plumbing.

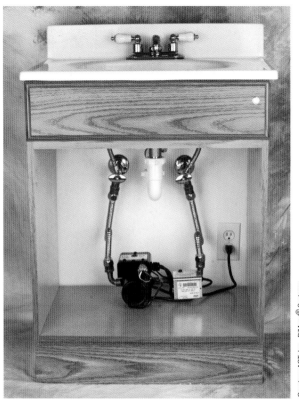

7-16 The pump and controls are installed below the most remote fixture.

hot water to the sink, and the cold water in the line moves back to the water heater. The pump and controls (7-16) are installed below the most remote fixture.

A variation of this system is to plumb the house so the hot water is a recirculating system (7-17). The pump and controller are mounted on the water heater, and hot water is circulated through a loop piping system. Since no water is wasted and it is returned to the water heater, any heat in it is not wasted. This produces water and energy savings.

WATER TREATMENT

Everyone is concerned about the purity of the drinking water. Whether it is from a well or a municipal water system, it is important that you be assured that the water is free of pollutants. You can have water samples tested to ascertain their purity. Standards are governed by the federal Safe Water Drinking Act, which is administered by the U.S. Environmental Protec-

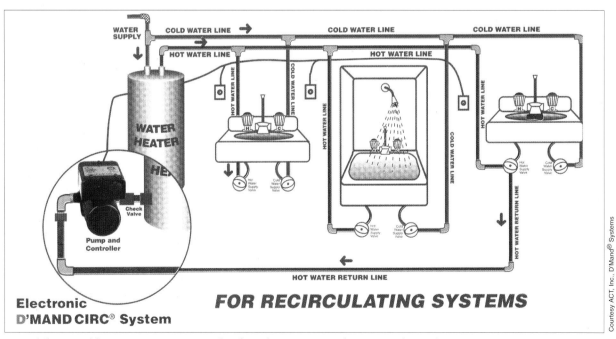

7-17 This rapid hot water system uses plumbing loops to provide a recirculating hot water system.

tion Agency and state health laws. To obtain information see "Additional Information," on page 155, for addresses.

Before you buy a water treatment unit, get information from the local public water and health departments concerning the quality of the water supplied. You can have private well water tested to find out what it contains that may need removing. Once you have this information you can begin to select a purification unit. No single unit removes all contaminants, so you need to choose one that will best suit your situation.

It is recommended you have the water from a private well tested once a year. It is best to test samples taken in the spring or summer following a rainy period. Also test after installing a new pump, having work done on the well, or replacing old pipes. Of course, always test the water from a new well.

Some of the contaminants often found in drinking water are chlorine, cryptosporidium, lead, radon, and nitrates. Lead gets into the water through the use of lead pipes still found in some older homes and lead solder used to connect copper pipe and brass fittings. This is a very dangerous situation. Radon and nitrates are found in the ground water.

Other contaminants include pesticides from runoff in agricultural areas, trichloroethylene from industrial effluents, and various bacteria and viruses that can appear in water that has not been properly disinfected or filtered.

WATER TREATMENT SYSTEMS

Two sources of information are the National Sanitation Foundation (NSF) and the Water Quality Association (WQA). The NSF develops standards and testing programs for home water treatment units as well as other consumer and industrial products. The WQA represents firms and individuals engaged in the production, sale, and services providing quality water. See also "Additional Information," on page 155, for addresses.

There are various in-home water treatment systems available. The following describes some of them. Before selecting one, check carefully to be certain it will remove the contaminants you expect. Also observe how much water they treat per minute. If you treat only water at the kitchen sink, ice maker, or chilled drinking water, a lower-volume unit can be chosen. Also consider how often you have to replace the filtering material and what this will cost.

ACTIVATED CARBON FILTERS

One type uses an activated carbon filter. Normal water pressure forces the water through canisters filled with activated carbon. The carbon filters may be granular, powdered, powder-coated paper, or pressed carbon black (7-18). The carbon filters trap the contaminating substances.

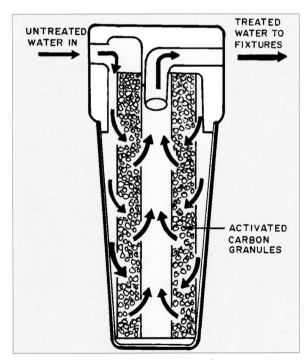

7-18 An activated carbon water purification system filters the incoming water through a granular carbon cartridge from which it flows to the faucet.

Some have a filter on the inflow side to remove sediment before it reaches the activated charcoal filter. This type of filter will remove some organic contaminants that cause undesirable tastes, odors, and colors. Some inorganic chemicals, such as chlorine, may be reduced. However, it will not remove most inorganic chemicals, suchas salts and metals. Some may remove lead, but you need to check this before buying. A filter should not be used alone on water containing harmful organisms. These require additional treatment.

Activated carbon systems deliver one-half to two or three gallons per minute. They will filter about 1000 gallons before you replace the carbon cartridge. Be certain to replace the carbon cartridge when required. A loaded cartridge will allow bacteria to collect and multiply. Follow the manufacturer's directions.

CERAMIC FILTERS

Another water filtration system uses a filtration unit with a replaceable ceramic cartridge that is mounted below the sink. The unit in **7-19** has a faucet with three handles: hot water, cold water, and pure filtered water. This third handle lets you run only the pure filtered water when you need it. The filtered water flows through a different waterway to the faucet than the normal hot and cold water thus eliminating possible contamination. The cartridge removes microscopic particles, cryptosporidium, lead, and chlorine. It will not treat microbiologically unsafe water.

DISTILLATION SYSTEMS

Distillation systems heat the incoming water in the tank with an electric heater until it turns to steam. This leaves the dissolved solids in the tank and they are drained away. The steam is run through a cooling coil, where it condenses into water and is drained to a storage tank. This process of distillation, however, does not remove volatile organic compounds. This is quite a slow process and produces very little water even after several hours of operation.

Courtesy Franke Consumer Products, Inc./Kitchen Systems Division

7-19 This water filtration system has a faucet with three handles: hot water, cold water, and pure filtered water. The filtration system is below the sink. It uses a replaceable ceramic cartridge.

REVERSE OSMOSIS

The reverse osmosis system forces the molecules of water through a membrane that traps the dissolved contaminants. These are drained away and the purified water is moved to a storage tank. It does use considerable water to wash away the contaminants so would increase your water bill. The membrane has to be replaced after it becomes clogged. The membranes are also subject to decay.

The treated water flows more slowly than the regular tap water.

ULTRAVIOLET DISINFECTION UNITS

These units destroy bacteria, deactivate viruses, and leave no taste or odor in the water. They are not effective in removing chemical pollutants.

The unit must be carefully maintained so dissolved and suspended solids in the water do not build up on the unit, blocking the ultraviolet light from reaching the water.

WATER SOFTENERS

Usually water obtained from a private well is classified as hard water because it has a high mineral content. This gives the water a taste different from that of water from a public utility water system where the water is processed before it is sent through the system.

Minerals in well water will stain plumbing fixtures a brown color, and the minerals will build up in the water heater and water distribution pipes. This will cause you to use more energy to heat water as the minerals build up, and eventually the heater will fail. The diameter of the water pipes will gradually be reduced until the flow is inadequate. All of these problems can be reduced by running the water through a water softener.

A typical water softener is shown in **7-20**. The untreated water enters through a canister containing a synthetic resin such as zeolite. The hard calcium and magnesium ions dissolved in the water are exchanged for soft sodium ions bonded to the resin. Once the resin is saturated with calcium and magnesium, it automatically flushes with salt water (called brine) from an adjoining tank containing salt and water. This regenerates the resin and the process repeats. The brine tank must be reloaded with salt on a regular schedule.

If you are on a low-sodium diet this may not be suitable for you because it leaves the water a bit salty. There are water softeners that are potassium-based, which may be better.

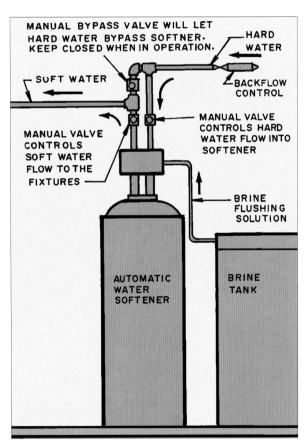

7-20 A water softener uses a synthetic resin to remove calcium and magnesium from the water. It uses a brine solution to flush the resin, regenerating it for continued use.

Kitchen Floors

Courtesy Wilsonart International

You have a wide choice of finish flooring materials suitable for use in a kitchen. The choice depends upon many factors, such as the atmosphere you are trying to achieve. For example, a warm wood floor (**8-1**) gives the room a totally different "look" and "feel" from ceramic tile or resilient floor covering (**8-2**). Your desire for a pattern or design will lead you to vinyl or possibly carpet. If you want to be able to mop the floor, this again leads you to consider the characteristics of the floor covering. Resilient floor covering washes easily while carpet requires special cleaners. If you plan to install the covering yourself you may not want to handle 12-foot-wide sheets of vinyl but choose 8- and 12-inch square tiles that are bonded to the floor with adhesives and are easy to cut and fit. Laminated wood tiles are also available.

8-1 This laminate wood floor covering gives a tough, durable surface and a warm atmosphere to the kitchen. The color of this example is harvest oak.

TABLE 8-1 COMMONLY USED UNDERLAYMENT MATERIALS

Resilient Floor Covering	Over old resilient floor if sound and flat Underlayment grade plywood, hardboard, or oriented strandboard	**Solid-Wood Flooring**	Over old wood flooring if sound and firmly attached Plywood or oriented strandboard subfloor
Ceramic Tile	Over old ceramic tile if it is firmly attached to subfloor Cement board Concrete slab	**Carpet**	Over any existing flooring provided it is sound and firmly attached All openings must be filled. If the preexisting flooring is in bad shape, cover with an underlayment such as plywood, hardboard, or oriented strandboard
High-Pressure Laminates	Over any existing flooring provided it is firmly secured to the subfloor		

FLOORING MATERIALS

Following are the more commonly used finish flooring materials and the underlayment materials used with them.

UNDERLAYMENT MATERIALS

Commonly used underlayment materials for various types of finish flooring are summarized in **Table 8-1**.

8-2 Resilient floor covering gives a durable surface that is easily cleaned and is available in a wide range of colors and patterns. This example shows a material giving a slight tan tint to the floor. It contributes to the bright atmosphere and complements the white cabinets.

Courtesy Congoleum Corporation

8-3 Brick pavers produce a durable floor but are very hard and not as pleasant to walk upon as wood, carpet, or resilient floor covering.

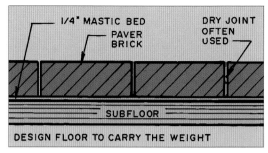

8-4 Brick pavers can be set on a plywood subfloor and bonded with a mastic.

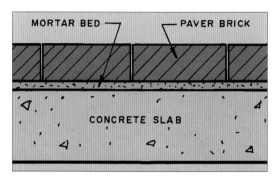

8-5 Brick pavers set on a concrete slab usually are set in a thin mortar bed.

8-6 While you can set pavers without mortar between the joints you can space them out and fill the joints with cement grout.

BRICK PAVERS

Brick pavers and brick flooring produce a hard, durable flooring. Pavers are thinner than standard brick and are usually preferred. Thickness ranges from 1¼ to 2¼ inches. Keep in mind that this thickness will raise the cabinets and appliances, so plan for this additional height (8-3). When set on a wood subfloor they are often set in a bed of mastic as shown in (8-4). They are set close together with a dry joint. If set on a concrete slab, mastic can also be used if the slab is absolutely flat. Usually this is not the case so a mortar bed is trowelled level and the brick pavers are set in it (8-5). A cement grout is usually placed in the joints between the pavers (8-6).

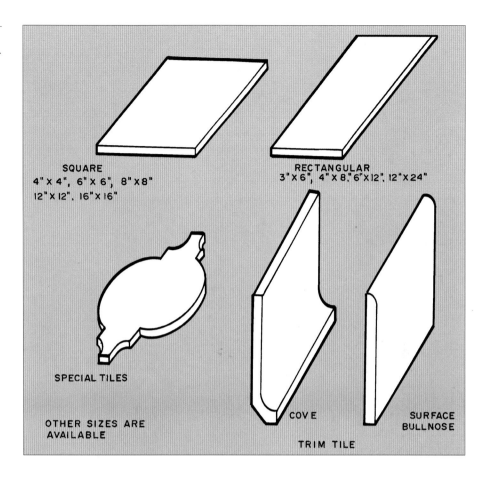

8-7 Typical sizes for the various types of clay floor tile. Consult the tile dealer for other sizes and special shapes available.

SQUARE
4"x 4", 6"x 6", 8"x8"
12"x 12", 16"x 16"

RECTANGULAR
3"x 6", 4"x 8," 6"x12", 12"x24"

SPECIAL TILES

OTHER SIZES ARE
AVAILABLE

COVE

SURFACE
BULLNOSE

TRIM TILE

CLAY TILE

Clay floor tile useful in kitchens includes ceramic tile, quarry tile, and paver tile.

The various types of clay floor tile are manufactured in a range of sizes and shapes. Commonly available sizes are shown in **8-7**.

Clay floor tile is hard, tough, durable and easy to clean. It is cold and can be slippery when wet. Some types have a slip resistant surface. It also reflects sound within the room. A cement grout is placed in the cracks between the tile, and this tends to darken and stain as the floor ages. However, it can be cleaned with readily available chemicals. Your dealer can show you grout samples from white to dark brown (**8-8**).

8-8 This ceramic floor tile has a dark brown grout providing a decorative feature. White and neutral grouts are available.

CERAMIC FLOOR TILE

Ceramic floor tile is a glazed product usually in 6-, 8-, 12-, and 16-inch squares. They are typically $\frac{5}{16}$-inch thick and laid with a ¼-inch space for grout (**8-9**). They can be bonded to an underlayment-grade plywood subfloor with mastic. However, it is highly recommended that a cement board underlayment be installed. The cement board is laid in a bed of adhesive recommended for this purpose and is screwed to the wood subfloor with bugle-head Phillips wood screws that have a noncorrosive coating. They are placed 4 inches apart on the edges of the panel and 12 inches apart on 16-inch centers on the interior of the panel. The joints are covered with fiberglass mesh drywall tape. It has an adhesive back so it is simply pressed onto the cement board. This keeps moisture from leaking to the wood subfloor below.

The cement board has a layer of mastic trowelled over the surface and the tiles are set in it. After it has cured, the spaces between the tile are filled with grout. As you work keep everything clean—your hands, the tile, and your tools.

The subfloor should be at least ¾ inch thick to reduce the possibility of deflection, which, if it occurs, will crack a tile or pull it loose (**8-10**).

Select a tile recommended by the manufacturer for use on floors. Typical wall tile will not usually take the wear that occurs on the floor. Some types have a slip-resistant surface.

Courtesy American Olean Tile Company

8-9 This floor is covered with 12-inch ceramic tiles set in mastic on a plywood subfloor. Notice how the color blends with the cabinets. The countertops and table have also been covered with ceramic tile.

Some ceramic floor tiles are ½- to ⅝-inch thick, so if you choose one of these you need to allow for this when you plan for installing appliances. Typically you should tile under the range, refrigerator, and dishwasher. The added thickness of the tile requires that you plan how it will abut the different flooring in an adjacent room. In **8-11** the transition was made with a marble threshold. In **8-12** a brass strip was placed over the union and secured to the subfloor.

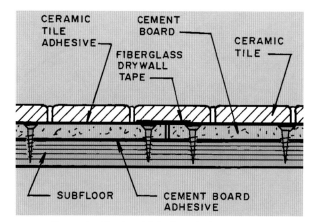

8-10 Ceramic tile should be bonded to a cement board underlayment that is nailed to the subfloor.

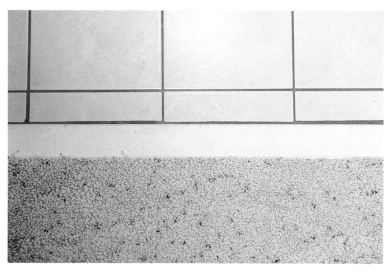

8-11 A marble threshold was placed at the door opening, allowing the ceramic tile to butt one side and the carpet in the next room the other side.

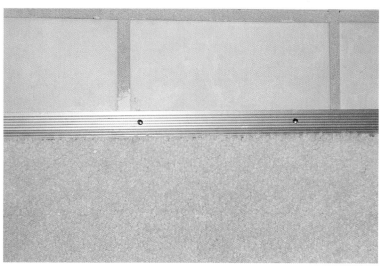

8-12 This brass strip was used to cover the joint between the ceramic tile and the carpet.

Should you want to try to save a little money you could lay underlayment under the appliances instead of installing tile. This underlayment must be the same thickness as the tile and be cut so it does not show around the edges of each of the appliances.

Quarry tile may be glazed or unglazed. They range in color from red to brown to buff. They are usually ½ to ¾ inch thick and come in squares, rectangles, and other shapes.

Paver tiles are standard-size unglazed tiles that resemble quarry tiles. They are usually 6 inches square or larger. They are waterproof and make a durable floor. They are installed in the same method as described for quarry tile. They are typically ⅜ to ½ inch thick.

Porcelain stone tile are made from refined ceramic materials and are a dense, highly stain-resistant, impervious product. The kitchen in **8-13** is finished with square tiles that are about ⁵⁄₁₆ inches thick. Notice the inlaid border provides an accent to the shape of the room. In **8-14** a different-colored tile is laid in the dining area surrounded by a sculpture porcelain stone border. This not only establishes the dining area but provides a wear-resistant surface.

Courtesy Crossville Ceramics Company

8-13 This kitchen floor is covered with porcelain stone tiles and accented with a stone border. It provides a durable easy to clean surface.

Courtesy Crossville Ceramics Company

8-14 This kitchen dining area is accented by a sculptured porcelain stone border and the mixing of two colors of tiles.

CARPET

Carpets are popular in kitchens because of the beauty and design, their sound-deadening properties, and the feeling of warmth. They do have the disadvantage of being difficult to clean, especially if food items are spilled on them. While carpets have a stain-resisting coating applied at the factory, they still stain rather easily. Furniture, such as chair legs, tend to dig into the carpet and leave indentations. While these can be worked out somewhat by rubbing with an ice cube, they still pose a problem (**8-15**).

Some types are much more suitable for kitchen use. Your carpet dealer can cite those available.

Following are several that could be considered. Of these it seems that **polypropylene fibers**, a class of olefin, is most often recommended (**8-16**). **Acrylic fibers** have good resistance to mildew, aging, sunlight, and chemicals.

8-15 This dining area in the end of the kitchen has been carpeted with an olefin fiber carpet.

8-16 Carpet in the kitchen gives a soft, comfortable working surface, deadens sound, and is available in a wide range of colors and patterns. This carpet was made using olefin fibers.

Modacrylic fibers are a form of the acrylic group. They also resist alkalis, acids, sunlight, and mildew. **Nylon fiber** is a strong fiber that is resistant to aging, mildew, and abrasion. It also has low moisture properties. **Polyropylene (olefin)** has the lowest moisture-absorption rate of all of these fibers. It also resists aging, mildew, abrasion, soiling, sunlight, and many household solvents.

RESILIENT FLOOR COVERINGS

Resilient floor covering includes materials that, while tough and firm, provide a degree of rebounding and return to the original form after being bent or compressed. Typical flooring products include vinyl and rubber. Sheet vinyl covering materials are polyvinyl chloride products that have a top layer of vinyl and a composition backing (**8-17**). Vinyl composition tiles are composed of vinyl resins, pigments, plasticizers, stabilizers, and fibers (**8-18**). Resilient sheet flooring is available in a wide range of colors and patterns and in a wood plank pattern (**8-19**).

Sheet vinyl composition floor covering is available in rolls 9 and 12 feet wide and up to 50 feet long. Thickness can vary from 0.069 to 0.224 inches, so check this before you buy it.

Vinyl composition tiles are available in 9-, 12-, 18-, and 36-inch squares and some rectangular shapes. Typical thicknesses of the tiles are ⅛ and 3/32 inch.

8-17 Resilient sheet flooring provides a durable, easy to install and clean finish flooring. This is one of the many colors and patterns available.

Courtesy Congoleum Corporation

8-18 Resilient floor tiles are easier for the home owner to install. The variety of colors and patterns enables you to select one that enhances your kitchen cabinets.

Courtesy Congoleum Corporation

Courtesy Congoleum Corporation

8-19 This resilient floor covering has a wood plank design and a natural wood color.

Vinyl flooring is bonded to the subfloor with the adhesive recommended by the flooring manufacturer. The adhesive is troweled on and the vinyl is laid over it, smoothed, and rolled with a heavy metal roller.

It is important that the subfloor be perfectly flat and smooth. If it is damaged, repair the damage, fill all holes and cracks, and drive in all nails sticking up. Better still, cover the old subfloor with plywood, hardboard, or oriented strandboard underlayment. Again, be certain no nail heads are above the surface and fill the cracks between the panels with crack filler. Any irregularities will eventually show through the resilient flooring.

WOOD FLOORING

There are several types of wood flooring frequently used in kitchens. The standard hardwood strip flooring has been used for years and is a fine product. A key to success is getting a hard, durable finish that will withstand the spills and the scraping of chair legs. Acrylic-impregnated and urethane top coatings are applied in the factory on prefinished flooring (**8-20**). Urethane is used on residential flooring, and acrylic, which is tougher, is used for residential and commercial applications. On-site

Courtesy Sub-Zero Freezer Co., Inc.

8-20 The stainless-steel refrigerator blends in with the acrylic-impregnated hardwood floor that resists spills and stains.

applications often are polyurethane, which may be oil-based or water-based. Oil-based polyurethane coatings take longer to dry and produce noxious fumes. They do penetrate deeper into the wood than water-based types. The water-based polyurethane coating dries rapidly and produces a hard finish. Both types provide good mar and abrasion resistance.

LAMINATE FLOORING

Laminate flooring is finding increasing use. It consists of a high-pressure plastic laminate outer surface over a medium-density fiberboard core. Laminate flooring is available in planks 7¼ inches wide and four feet long (8-21). It is also available

8-21 Laminate flooring has a high-pressure laminate surface bonded to a medium-density fiberboard core. They are tough and durable and have the appearance of solid-wood flooring.

Courtesy Wilsonart International

in 15½-inch square tiles (**8-22**). It can be laid over existing flooring such as wood, vinyl sheet and vinyl tile, and ceramic tile. It is a floating floor in that it is not nailed or glued to the sub-floor. The floor is covered with a special foam padding and the laminate pieces are laid over it (**8-23**). They have tongue-and-groove edges that are glued together (**8-24**).

8-22 This kitchen floor has been finished with high-pressure laminate flooring squares. Two different wood patterns were used to produce this checkerboard design.

Courtesy Wilsonart International

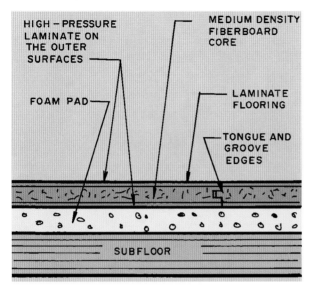

HIGH–PRESSURE
LAMINATE ON
THE OUTER
SURFACES

MEDIUM DENSITY
FIBERBOARD
CORE

FOAM PAD

LAMINATE
FLOORING

TONGUE AND
GROOVE
EDGES

SUBFLOOR

8-23 The high-pressure laminate flooring is laid over a special foam pad.

PREPARING
THE SUBFLOOR

If you have new construction the subfloor will be plywood, particleboard, or oriented strandboard. Each is a good product and if not damaged during construction will provide a sound base. Over this floor you will install an underlayment. This provides an even, smooth surface upon which the finish flooring is laid. The choice depends somewhat upon the type of finish flooring to be used.

Hardwood floors can be laid directly on the subfloor if it is sound, free of damage, and level. If it is not, you will have to fill any holes, cut away any ridges or bumps, and lay a ¼-inch underlayment of plywood or waferboard or oriented strandboard. Glue and nail it securely to the subfloor.

Ceramic tile is laid over ¼-inch-thick cement board. The sheets are securely nailed to the subfloor and the joists covered with tape.

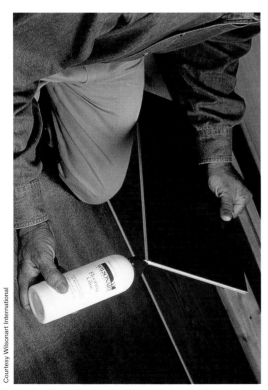

Courtesy Wilsonart International

1. Apply adhesive to the tongue-and-groove edge of the laminate flooring.

2. Press the piece into place and wipe off the excess adhesive on the surface.

8-24 The laminate flooring is bonded on the tongue-and-groove edges with an adhesive.

Vinyl floor covering is installed over ¼-inch plywood, oriented strandboard, or waferboard underlayment. It is especially important the surface be perfectly flat. Any small dent, hole, or ridge will show through the vinyl covering. Some fill the cracks between the sheets with crack filler. Set all nails flush with the surface, or sink and fill over the head.

Carpet is installed over the same underlayment as vinyl floor covering.

REMOVING OLD FLOORING MATERIALS

If you plan to cover old solid-wood flooring you can usually leave it. Nail it securely in place and repair damaged sections. Install an underlayment if it is in really bad shape.

Old resilient sheet and tile floor covering can be covered in some cases with a new flooring adhered to it if it is solidly bonded to the subfloor. Let your flooring dealer advise you on this decision. Usually it is preferred to remove the old resilient material. Remember very old resilient covering could be asphalt tiles or sheets, linoleum or products that have some asbestos. Some of the backing materials may have deteriorated. Technically this should be removed by a professional trained and equipped to handle asbestos dust particles. If you try removing it wear a mask, respirator, eye protection, long sleeves and a hat. In any case you are taking a chance if you have a lot of deterioration in the old covering if it contains asbestos.

Begin by removing the quarter-round molding along the baseboard covering the edge of the flooring. If you plan to reuse it, number it so you remember where it goes.

If you have sheet material, cut it across the room in strips 8 to 10 inches wide. Pry up one corner and peel the strip off the subfloor. If it is tightly bonded, scrape it loose with a long-handled scraper. When all is moved go back over the subfloor, rescraping any small pieces remaining and removing old adhesive.

If the sheet material is really stuck hard you can rent an electric hot air blower and play it on the surface until the adhesive softens. Your home hair dryer will work on small areas.

Resilient tiles are removed in much the same way. Use a 4-inch-wide hand scraper and pry up a corner. Use heat if necessary and scrape up each tile.

In all cases wear eye protection and heavy gloves. Long sleeves and full-length trousers are recommended.

Removing old damaged solid-wood flooring is a big job. You will need a good strong pry bar and a hammer. You can force the bar under the flooring and pry it up. As it rises you can often get a bar on a nail and pull it out. You can also cut the strips into shorter lengths. Cut through the flooring with a portable circular saw but do not cut the subfloor. Watch out for nails. You will most likely hit one sooner or later.

Old ceramic tile is removed as described by resilient tile. You will most likely have to hammer on the pry bar to break the tile loose. Remember, tile will shatter, so protect yourself from the shards that may fly about.

Before you install the underlayment clean the subfloor. A good rough sweeping followed by vacuuming is necessary. If possible use a shop vacuum, because it is much stronger than the typical home vacuum. Some installers spray a light mist of water over the subfloor to try to control the dust as they vacuum. Any dust left will reduce the bonding strength of the adhesive with the new flooring.

If you are installing a finish floor over a concrete slab it must be clean and level. If it is irregular or damaged, get a latex surface preparation material from your building supply store and trowel it over the defects and level low spots. Remember, if the concrete slab shows evidence of moisture penetration you must control this before installing any finish floor.

Additional Information

The National Kitchen and Bath Association is a professional organization representing over 7,000 industry professionals across the U.S. and Canada, including manufacturers, dealers, designers, products, etc. Related publications are available from:

National Kitchen and Bath Association
687 Willow Grove St.
Hackettstown, NJ 07840-9988
800-843-6522, www.nkba.org.

Specifications for making buildings accessible by the physically handicapped are in the report *ANSI-A117.1,* produced by and available from:

American National Standards Institute, Inc.
11 West 42nd St., 13th Floor
New York, NY 10036

The *Americans with Disabilities Act,* and *Guidelines* are available from:

U.S. Architectural & Transportation Barriers Compliance Board
1331 F Street N.W., Suite 1000
Washington, DC 20004-1111

Other trade organizations and government agencies that may be helpful include:

Kitchen Cabinet Manufacturers Association
1899 Preston White Drive
Reston, VA 22091

National Association of Home Builders
1201 Fifteenth St. NW
Washington, DC 20005

National Sanitation Foundation
P.O. Box 1468
Ann Arbor, MI 48106

Resilient Floor Covering Institute
966 Hungerford Dr., Suite 12B
Rockville, MD 20850

Lighting Research Institute
120 Wall St., 17th Floor
New York, NY 10005

U.S. Environmental Protection Agency
Office of Drinking Water
401 M St. SW,
Washington, DC 20460

Water Quality Association
P.O. Box 606
Lisle, IL 60532

Selected Bibliography

DeChiara, J., J. Panero, and M. Zelnick. *Time-Saver Standards for Interior Design and Space Planning;* New York: McGraw-Hill, 1984.

———— *Time Saver Standards for Housing and Residential Development;* New York: McGraw-Hill, 1984.

Merritt, F.S. and J.T. Ricketts. *Building Design and Construction Handbook;* New York: McGraw-Hill, 1994.

Spence, W.P. *Carpentry & Bulding Construction;* New York: Sterling Publishing Co., 1999.

Spence, W.P. *Finish Carpentry;* New York: Sterling Publishing Co., 1995.

Sweet's General Building and Renovation, Catalog File; New York: McGraw-Hill.

Sweet's Group, *Kitchen and Bath Source Book;* New York: McGraw-Hill.

Index

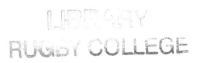

Metric Equivalents

[to the nearest mm, 0.1cm, or 0.01m]

inches	mm	cm	inches	mm	cm	inches	mm	cm
⅛	3	0.3	13	330	33.0	38	965	96.5
¼	6	0.6	14	356	35.6	39	991	99.1
⅜	10	1.0	15	381	38.1	40	1016	101.6
½	13	1.3	16	406	40.6	41	1041	104.1
⅝	16	1.6	17	432	43.2	42	1067	106.7
¾	19	1.9	18	457	45.7	43	1092	109.2
⅞	22	2.2	19	483	48.3	44	1118	111.8
1	25	2.5	20	508	50.8	45	1143	114.3
1¼	32	3.2	21	533	53.3	46	1168	116.8
1½	38	3.8	22	559	55.9	47	1194	119.4
1¾	44	4.4	23	584	58.4	48	1219	121.9
2	51	5.1	24	610	61.0	49	1245	124.5
2½	64	6.4	25	635	63.5	50	1270	127.0
3	76	7.6	26	660	66.0			
3½	89	8.9	27	686	68.6			

inches	feet	m
4	102	10.2	28	711	71.1
4½	114	11.4	29	737	73.7	12	1	0.31
5	127	12.7	30	762	76.2	24	2	0.61
6	152	15.2	31	787	78.7	36	3	0.91
7	178	17.8	32	813	81.3	48	4	1.22
8	203	20.3	33	838	83.8	60	5	1.52
9	229	22.9	34	864	86.4	72	6	1.83
10	254	25.4	35	889	88.9	84	7	2.13
11	279	27.9	36	914	91.4	96	8	2.44
12	305	30.5	37	940	94.0	108	9	2.74

Conversion Factors

1 mm	=	0.039 inch	1 inch	=	25.4 mm	mm	=	millimeter
1 m	=	3.28 feet	1 foot	=	304.8 mm	cm	=	centimeter
1 m²	=	10.8 square feet	1 square foot	=	0.09 m²	m	=	meter
						m²	=	square meter